iolo williams
Wild about the Wild

iolo williams
Wild about the Wild

Gomer

First impression 2005

ISBN 1 84323 458 0

© text: Iolo Williams
© photographs: Iolo Williams
   (unless noted otherwise)

Iolo Williams has asserted his right under the Copyright, Designs and Patents Act, 1988 to be identified as author of this work.

All rights reserved. No part of this book may be reproduced, stored in a retrieval system, or transmitted in any form or by any means, electronic, electrostatic, magnetic tape, mechanical, photocopying, recording or otherwise without permission in writing from the publishers, Gomer Press, Llandysul, Ceredigion, Wales.

Designed by Stephen Paul Dale.

The Publisher acknowledges the financial support of the Welsh Books Council.

Printed in Wales at Gomer Press, Llandysul, Ceredigion.

This book is dedicated to my beautiful wife, Ceri,

and my two wonderful boys, Dewi and Tomos.

IOLO WILLIAMS

ACKNOWLEDGEMENTS

I am particularly indebted to my *taid*, mum and dad who walked patiently, for hundreds of miles, with a young naturalist whose thirst for knowledge was unquenchable. For their patience, kindness and love, I will always be grateful. I would also like to thank those Welsh naturalists who influenced me and a whole host of other birdwatchers and botanists from my generation, and I am grateful to my colleagues from the early years with the RSPB in Wales, who were always very supportive.
It would not have been possible to undertake so many great adventures in one calendar year without the assistance of so many knowledgable companions and friends – I thank you all. I would also like to thank Dyfed Elis-Gruffydd for his invaluable comments, and all at Gwasg Gomer, especially Ceri Wyn Jones, for all their hard work in putting this book together.

CONTENTS

VIII **INTRODUCTION**

 1 **SEPTEMBER**
Conkers and Councils

 19 **OCTOBER**
Hunting and Sprooting

 37 **NOVEMBER**
Guy Fawkes and Costa Rica

 55 **DECEMBER**
Taiwan and Llyn Tegid

 73 **JANUARY**
Turkey to Talgarth

 91 **FEBRUARY**
Colombo to Caernarfon

 109 **MARCH**
St David and the Apes

 127 **APRIL**
Turtles and Dragons

 145 **MAY**
Sun, Swans and Snakes

 163 **JUNE**
Mad Dogs and Merlins

 181 **JULY**
Elvis and the Hobbies

 199 **AUGUST**
Alaska and the Eisteddfod

INTRODUCTION

As a young man, I remember being enthralled by Gilbert White's famous book *The Natural History of Selbourne*. In it, he chronicles the wealth of wildlife found in the countryside around his home more than two centuries ago. I was fascinated by the huge changes that have occurred in the British landscape between White's time and the present-day, and I became determined to record the natural history surrounding my own home here in mid Wales. This book chronicles a wildlife year in my life, from September 2004 until the end of August 2005. It was, without doubt, an exciting year with overseas expeditions to Indonesia to see the infamous Komodo dragons and to Uganda to film mountain gorillas. It was a joyous year: the Welsh rugby team won a memorable Grand Slam with a flair that we associate with the great team of the 1970s. But it was also a tragic year: who can forget the Asian tsunami that killed tens of thousands of people in the Far East? However, when I look back at the year, it will be most memorable for the subtle changes that occur day after day and week after week in the Welsh countryside, from the arrival of the first swallow to the falling of autumn leaves. I hope you enjoy reading the book but more than that, I hope it will provide future generations with an insight into the natural history of Wales and other parts of the world during the early years of the twenty-first century.

iolo williams | conker and councils

CONKERS AND COUNCILS

'If this wonderful weather continues, I'll have a tan to replace the one washed away by the August rains! Anyway, as I drove the boys to school today, a covey of red-legged partridges exploded from the roadside verge.'

WREN (photo: Steve Phillipps)

SEPTEMBER

September 1st There isn't a cloud in the sky and a full moon is still visible as the sun rises over the horizon. Still, it must have been a cold night last night because when I took the dogs for their early morning walk around the field, the leaves and berries of the elder tree in the corner of the field were dripping with morning dew. The spiders' webs glistened in the bright sunlight and only a blind and foolish insect would have stumbled into these.

The nuthatch is noisy once more on an old ash tree that overlooks the garden. He's been quiet since he reared his brood in a secure hole left behind by a rotting oak branch but now he's back with a vengeance, advertising his presence with his sharp call and even sharper, dagger-like bill. Of all the birds that visit the garden, he has to be the most intolerant. Indeed, any great tit or chaffinch within pecking distance risks losing an eye. Still, it's nice to see him back.

September 2nd A second beautiful day – but I'm stuck in a car on the way to Cardiff! Still, the sight of a stunning flock of linnets on a thistled field near Llandrindod Wells makes the drive worthwhile.

Each time I visit Cardiff, I'm amazed by the acres of greenery within the city limits. Bute Park, within spitting distance of the Millennium Stadium, is one of the best places I know to see shy species such as jays and kingfishers, two of our most stunning birds. Today, the jays were out in force, taking advantage of one particular oak that was heavy with acorns. I watched one individual hide over half a dozen in a small hole in the wall of Cardiff Castle with dozens of tourists, a few metres away, completely oblivious to its presence. I doubt whether the acorns will still be there come the winter as I spied another interested observer on a branch above the tourists: a young grey squirrel!

September 3rd If this wonderful weather continues, I'll have a tan to replace the one washed away by the August rains! Anyway, as I drove the boys to school today, a covey of red-legged partridges exploded from the roadside verge.

It's almost twenty years since I last saw the native grey partridge in this part of mid Wales, and over five years since I saw this species anywhere in Wales. The decline in mixed farming and gamekeeping has made it a rare bird here, but it holds its own in some parts of south-east England where it's shot as game. A few years back, I spoke to an old railwayman who told me that he'd often find partridge nests in the tall vegetation along the verges of the railway line that ran between Caersws and Llanidloes. That line, like the grey partridges and the old railwayman, has long since gone.

September 4th A dull, overcast day – I knew it was too good to last!

This year, the hazel trees are heavy with nuts, to such an extent that even the grey squirrels haven't been able to cope with the harvest of plenty. Usually, they gobble up the nuts before I can get at them, but last night,

when I went for a walk with the dogs along the country lane which passes our house, I was afforded the luxury of as many nuts (and blackberries) as I could manage! Indeed, many of our trees are overladen with fruits and seeds this year, from the elder and horse chestnut to the rowan and hawthorn. Weather permitting, it should be an easy autumn for many of our small mammals and birds.

Surely there can be no more fragrant a flower than the honeysuckle. As I walked along the lane last night, its sweet scent was everywhere. The honeysuckle is a climbing plant with greyish leaves and is particularly common in healthy hedgerows. The scent is at its strongest at night in order to attract moths, which feed on the plentiful nectar and carry pollen from one plant to the next. As a child, I remember picking the

GREY SQUIRREL

flowers to suck the sugary nectar from the base, a useful source of energy when I found myself miles from home with no food or drink.

In the afternoon, I went down to Newtown with my two sons to watch the local rugby and cricket teams playing. Towards the end of the cricket match, a pair of mute swans in their dazzling 'whites' flew low over the wickets, momentarily bringing play to an awestruck halt.

September 5th A fine, misty morning so I decided to go for a run along the banks of the Montgomeryshire Canal with the dogs. Built between 1774 and 1821 to carry limestone from quarries at Llanymynech and to ferry wool, meat and other agricultural produce to the Midlands, it hasn't seen a longboat for over half a century. However, man's loss is nature's gain and over the years, it's become a linear refuge for a wide variety of wildlife.

This morning, I came across a female tufted duck with three well-grown young, the first time I've encountered this species on the canal. They generally nest in tall vegetation around the shores of shallow, lowland ponds and keep to open water over the winter months. They are diving ducks, the male a glossy black with white flanks and belly, the female a dull brown because she's the one who will have to rely on her camouflage to incubate her 7 to 12 eggs.

I'm not a born athlete but I do enjoy my jaunts along the canal and this morning, I was reminded of how you can use your ears to distinguish between various birds as they take flight. Mallards and other ducks fly

HISSING SID, THE MUTE SWAN

off the water in a cacophony of sound, much as a woodpigeon does in the branches of a tree. Moorhens, on the other hand, either run frantically along the surface of the water with flailing wings or dive underwater with a distinct 'plop', resurfacing again only when they reach the safety of the tall vegetation along the canal banks. Herons take to the skies with their slow, deep wingbeats, an occasional 'kraak' call often the only indication that they were there at all. Mute swans, however, merely stare regally, reminding me that I'm the one who should be moving along!

September 6th The view out of the bathroom window at seven this morning was stunning as the mist in the valley meandered its way towards the English border like a wide river of cotton wool.

I spent a wonderful morning in the company of Tony Cross of the Welsh Kite Trust. Tony is one of those exceptional ornithologists who undertakes a phenomenal amount of fieldwork every year. Unfortunately, such hands-on experts are an endangered species amongst conservation organisations where more and more pen-pushers are appointed to key roles.

This morning, I accompanied him to ring a brood of five cygnets on the Montgomeryshire Canal near the hamlet of Aberbechan, a pilgrimage which Tony has carried out each year for the past decade. The cob, or male swan, is particularly aggressive and is known locally as 'Hissing Sid' because of his habit of attacking passers-by as they tread the Severn Way footpath. Today, Sid was not his usual boisterous self because he had moulted all his flight feathers and we were therefore able to catch, ring and weigh all five youngsters with relative ease.

Because of his long-term study, Tony has been able to follow some of 'his' birds for several years and it would appear that many of the youngsters from mid Wales spend their first few years of life on estuaries such as Aberogwen near Bangor. They are generally between 3 and 5 years old before they are able to establish a territory near their natal area, but few make it this far. Over half will have died, many from collisions with overhead power lines and predation by foxes, but those that succeed in reaching breeding age can live to be over 20 years of age.

September 7th There are wasps everywhere this year! I don't think I've ever seen so many. This is due in part to the mild winter resulting in many of the queens surviving until spring, but also the dry weather throughout the early summer will have made it ideal for breeding. Every

day now, I release a dozen or more from the house and although they usually become aggressive during the autumn as they seek out sugary liquids, this is the first year for a long time that I haven't been stung – not yet at least!

It has also been a good year for the robin's pincushion. This is an incredible red, cotton wool-like structure that you find near the tip of dog rose branches. It's actually caused by a wasp, *Diplolepis rosae* to give it its full name, which lays its eggs on the branch. The larva then burrows into the tissue, causing the plant to go haywire and send out a ball of small filaments which protects the developing insect until an adult wasp emerges the following spring.

September 8th & 9th Two glorious days' filming around Yr Eifl, a mountain near the eastern end of the Llŷn peninsula. The sun shone constantly and choughs, rare red-beaked and red-legged crows, were constant companions.

When the weather is at its best, it's difficult to beat north-west Wales for scenery and wildlife. On Yr Eifl itself, we watched stonechats strutting their stuff on the tops of gorse bushes and a female kestrel spent the best

ROBIN'S PINCUSHION

part of an afternoon hunting beetles and voles amongst the heather. Offshore, porpoises torpedoed through the water, no doubt chasing the same schools of mackerel as the huge, white gannets. On one isolated beach, a female grey seal had given birth and while she diligently nursed her offspring, a huge bull waited in the shallows.

September is the month when most grey seals give birth in Welsh waters and although the bulk of the population can be found around the rugged coastline of south-west Wales, an increasing number breed around the Llŷn peninsula. The mother's milk contains up to 60% fat and on this diet, the pup doubles its weight in the first week. During this period, the female doesn't feed and she loses weight rapidly until, at about 17 weeks, she abandons the pup. The youngster then has to learn to fend for itself, living initially off the thick layer of blubber that also acts as an insulator.

September 10th I went to Llanberis to help launch Gwynedd's biodiversity action plan, basically a plan to conserve and enhance the county's flora and fauna. As part of the launch, we went on a boat trip around Llyn Padarn in the pouring rain, but despite the weather we saw a few cormorants, coots and goosanders.

We were also shown two dead Arctic char, or *torgoch* as it's known in Welsh. This fish was left behind in some of Snowdonia's deepest lakes by the last Ice Age and although it lives in the colder water near the bottom, it comes to the shallows each December to spawn. The male is a beautiful creature with its dark green back and bright orange-red belly, but the female, as is the case with its close relative the salmon, is silvery-grey. At the end of the day, I'm not ashamed to admit that I took both fish away to be eaten, and very tasty they were too.

September 12th Although most birds gave up singing over two months ago, the wrens are still in fine voice in the hedge surrounding our house. This morning, I listened to two males sparring for almost an hour, neither willing to yield to its opponent. For a small bird, the wren has a tremendous voice which, on a still morning, can carry for hundreds of metres. Last year, I found a wren's nest containing well-feathered young on August 30th and one of the calling birds in my hedge is still feeding young reared in an ivy-covered poplar nearby.

Wrens are our commonest breeding birds with over seven million pairs in Great Britain. They can be found from the seashore to the highest mountain and I recall finding a pair feeding young in a nest within a stone's throw of the top of Snowdon. Their worst enemy is the cold and there were significant declines during the atrocious winter weather of 1962-63. Since 1981, however, the winters have been relatively mild and the wren has taken full advantage to colonise virtually every available habitat.

September 13th Back down to the Cardiff area for three days' filming. Today, it was the turn of Caerphilly Castle where the moat provides an ideal home for mute swans, coots, moorhens and two species of feral geese, the greylag and Canadian. A late sedge warbler, still to depart for Africa, skulked in the reeds fringing the moat and flocks of swallows and house martins made the most of the thousands of insects hugging the water's surface. Whilst seeking shelter from one of the many heavy showers, I found that I was sharing my temporary accommodation beneath a bramble-infested elder with a male blackbird which had fluffed out its feathers and tucked itself beneath a particularly broad bramble leaf. Had I searched high and low for hours on end, I doubt that I could have come up with a drier, more secure location than that chosen by the wily blackbird.

September 14th The cockney sparrow is, by all accounts, disappearing from former haunts all over London. A recent survey has shown that it is virtually extinct in many of the London boroughs and even the parks no longer support the burgeoning populations of the past. The exact reasons are not known but various theories have been put forward and one well-known daily newspaper has even put up a reward for the first scientist who comes up with the definitive answer to what must surely be a very complex problem.

In Cardiff market, however, the house sparrow is still doing rather well, at least that's how it appeared to me this morning as I watched a flock of nearly 20 birds squeeze their way through a broken window into the market hall. What attracted them was a pet-food stall that had unwisely placed several bins full of bird seed, without their lids, within easy reach of the birds.

It was comical to watch. The sparrows would fly down to feed unmolested until the stall owner walked over to chase them away. The birds would then retreat to the roof of the market hall where they stayed for several minutes until the owner was distracted by a customer. Once this happened, the birds would fly down once more as the whole cycle started over again. In the meantime, I was supposed to be concentrating on learning my lines.

September 15th When I arrived home this evening, I took the boys down to the nearby graveyard! Why? Conkers! It is a spot surrounded by four huge horse chestnuts and this year, they are laden with conkers. It's still a week or two early to collect most of them but one or two spiky cases had fallen to the ground following the high winds of the past week.

I still feel that child-like excitement every time I open the casing and stare at the chestnut brown of a fresh conker. As kids, we'd try to pickle them, roast them and cover them in dung in an attempt to produce the perfect conker. All my attempts ended in failure but nonetheless, the schoolyard in late September and early October was always strewn with the debris of teenage conker wars. In those days, we had to climb the trees and shake the branches to get at the hallowed seeds but today, in the age of play-stations and cartoon channels, conkers galore lie unwanted on lawns and roadsides all over Britain.

September 16th Wouldn't it be fascinating to set up a camera on the lawn outside your house to see exactly which animals visit once we're all tucked up in bed for the night? I can't imagine that many gardens aren't visited by a fox at some time or other and you'd expect to see hedgehogs and possibly badgers. Some, I'm sure, will have more unusual visitors such as deer, otter and polecat although dogs and cats tend to keep the more timid creatures away. Who knows, you could even be lucky enough to see the elusive pine marten which is now extremely rare in Wales, or even a panther if recent newspaper reports are to be believed. On second thoughts, it's probably best that we don't know what goes on in our gardens after dark!

This afternoon, I took the dogs for a walk through the mixed woodland at the back of the house. The track that bisects the wood is quite well-used by walkers but the recent storms have felled an ivy-covered hazel tree which has now provided an ideal plucking post for a sparrowhawk. These birds of prey are well-adapted for life in the woods, their short, broad wings and long tails allowing them to weave in and out of the trees at high speeds. They regularly use favoured spots such as tree stumps or large rocks as 'plucking posts', where they pull most of the feathers from their victims before devouring the flesh.

This sparrowhawk's latest victim is a woodpigeon, its tri-banded tail feathers very evident amongst the pile of debris. My guess is that the perpetrator is a female as the smaller male would struggle to overcome a bird as heavy as a woodpigeon. His prey usually consists of small passerines such as tits, chaffinches and thrushes, many of which are taken in gardens.

September 17th I read in today's paper that one of Wales's rarest seabirds, the little tern, has had a successful breeding season at its last remaining colony at Gronant near Prestatyn. When I first worked for the RSPB in the early 1980s, there were five colonies scattered around the

PEREGRINE FALCON

wild about the wild | **conkers and councils**

coast from Tywyn in Merionnydd to Gronant. All bar one of the colonies have now disappeared.

Protecting such a species is hard work. By the time the terns arrive back in Wales from their West African wintering quarters in May, a temporary fence will have been erected around the breeding area and as soon as the first birds lay eggs, an electric fence will be erected. For the following two months, the terns will be protected around the clock by paid wardens and an army of volunteers.

Why go to such extremes to protect one species at one site? To begin with, it is Wales's last remaining colony and if these birds go, another species will be wiped off the Welsh slate. Also, little terns are one of the avian world's 'Mars bars' because virtually every predator eats either the birds themselves or their eggs and young. They are targeted by hedgehogs, stoats, weasels, polecats, foxes, at least four different types of crow, kestrels, gulls and peregrine falcons.

Nests on the sandy spit are constantly under threat from high tides and those humans walking their dogs or in four-wheel-drive vehicles. The scarcer the birds become, the more likely they are to fall foul of that oddest breed of kleptomaniacs, the egg collectors. All in all, it's no wonder that so much effort goes into protecting one small bird, and with 167 chicks fledged in 2004, the colony is going from strength to strength.

September 18th The family ventured out between the morning rain showers to gather the last few blackberries before they disappear for another year. It's been a particularly good harvest this autumn and we found plenty of evidence to show that we weren't the only animals to have taken advantage of this annual treat. Badger droppings in a nearby latrine were dark purple in colour as was a fox scat along the woodland edge.

While we were gathering the berries, we disturbed several red admirals, surely one of our most striking butterflies with their black wings and bold red and white patterns. We watched closely as they unfurled their long proboscis, a kind of tubular mouthpart, to suck nutrients from the over-ripe blackberries. When they finished eating, the proboscis was stored away once more, curled up beneath the chin.

Red admirals are migratory species that arrive in Britain from Africa and continental Europe throughout the spring and summer. Females lay

their eggs on nettles and by the summer, there will be a fresh emergence of butterflies. These will continue to fly until October or, on sunny days, even into November and exceptionally, I have seen some as late as mid-December. With the winters becoming milder, an increasing number of adults overwinter in the south of England but I have yet to record this here in mid Wales.

Incidentally, the blackberries made an excellent crumble.

September 19th A leisurely morning in the house with the boys, much of it spent catching spiders. Although we've only been in our new home a year, the large house spiders have already found us and made their homes in every available nook and cranny. I like spiders. They eat all kinds of insects from bluebottles to houseflies to midges, and any creature that eats the mosquitoes which settle in our house every autumn will always receive a warm welcome.

My wife used to be quite phobic about them but now, thanks to a gradual education programme, she's much more tolerant. She would never dream of picking one up but they are now allowed to live unmolested in our house as long as they don't crawl over our bed at night. The boys love them, as most kids do. To them, they are not yet the stuff of nightmares and horror films, merely 'cool' creatures that kill and devour flies.

September 20th A sad day because, this afternoon, we buried Ros Tudor, a colleague of mine at the RSPB for almost 15 years. Ros was a real wildlife enthusiast and the lynchpin of a very successful RSPB Wales team during the 1980s and 1990s.

BLACKBERRIES

wild about the wild | conkers and councils

Having left the funeral in a rather melancholy mood, I nipped home to fetch my binoculars and headed over to Dolydd Hafren, a gem of a nature reserve in the Severn valley near Welshpool. Managed by the Montgomeryshire Wildlife Trust, the reserve encompasses several fields, oxbow lakes and the confluence of the rivers Rhiw, Camlad and Severn. It's one of the few sites I know that is worth a visit at any time of the year because the flow of the river, the migrant birds, the light and the very mood of the place are constantly changing.

As I arrived, a male bullfinch called from an elder overhanging the car park and several woodpigeons shot out from an adjacent hawthorn. All along the footpath to the two hides, the native bushes were heavy with berries and fruits. Most prominent amongst them were the bright red berries of the guelder-rose and the unique fruits of the spindle. Here and there, groups of tree sparrows called from the thick hedgerows but try as I might, I could not entice them out into the open. This species has declined by almost 90% in the past 25 years, but thanks to the work of the local wildlife trust they are flourishing here at Dolydd Hafren.

Sitting in the comfort of a hide overlooking the river Severn and two of the oxbow lakes, my gloom rapidly gave way to celebration as I

GUELDER-ROSE

watched little egrets, teal, mallard, goosander, heron, snipe, a female peregrine, two buzzards, three hares; the list is a long one. This was the perfect antidote to a sad day.

Two hours later, as I walked slowly back towards the car, a shaft of sunlight finally broke through the wall of dark clouds, illuminating a solitary red poppy in a recently cut field of corn. A fitting tribute to Ros, a colleague and a friend.

September 21st On the way back from Cardiff to mid Wales, I visited the Gwent Wildlife Trust's Silent Valley reserve on the outskirts of the village of Cwm near Ebbw Vale. What a fantastic place! The main part of the reserve consists of an ancient beech woodland but it also has areas of wet grassland and mixed woodland. On my brief visit, I saw several green woodpeckers, a bird that has become remarkably scarce in most of north and west Wales. With its red cap, black face, green back and large size it is very distinctive, although the greenish-yellow youngsters are often mistaken for the much rarer golden oriole.

It's quite remarkable how many people still believe that the south Wales valleys are full of nothing more than coal slag and polluted rivers. It's true that thousands of acres of prime wildlife habitat were desecrated in order to extract the black gold, but nearly all the valleys still contain pristine broadleaved woodlands or unspoiled bracken-covered hillsides. These are among the best places in Wales to see many birds that have declined elsewhere, species such as tree pipits, yellowhammers and kestrels.

September 22nd I come back home after a day's filming and find to my horror that Powys County Council have cut the hedge along the narrow lane leading to our house – for the third time this year! When I walked that same lane two days ago, I counted at least twelve robin's pincushions; this evening, they have all been destroyed.

I do not understand the council's obsession with tidiness. They are constantly whinging about a lack of funding for health and education and yet, in spite of the complaints of the local wildlife trust and local people, they continue to waste tens of thousands of pounds by needlessly cutting roadside verges and hedges three or four times a year. And all this 12 years after they committed themselves to the conservation of Powys's wildlife in the wake of the Rio summit!

wild about the wild | conkers and councils

In Powys, as in many other authorities across Wales, it seems that councillors weren't in class on the day that God handed out common sense!

One plant to have escaped the destruction was the dog rose with its large berries called rose hips. As kids, we would use the hairy seeds inside the pods as itching powder and my mother remembers boiling the berries during the war to make a Ribena-type drink rich in vitamin C. This was a time when food, and fresh foods in particular, were in very short supply and therefore children were often paid to collect tens of thousands of rose hips from hedgerows all over Britain.

September 23rd Following heavy rain throughout the night, the river Severn is a brown torrent this morning. Indeed, the water level is higher than it's been since the end of the winter and the kingfishers that I've seen regularly over the past few weeks have gone, probably to some quieter backwaters where the fishing is easier. Cormorants, however, appear to like the high water and three were fishing the same deep pool on the outskirts of Newtown.

When I used to fish for trout in the river Efyrnwy near the village of Llanwddyn, the experienced fishermen always believed that the fish were easier to catch following a rainstorm because an abundance of earthworms and grubs would be washed down the river along with all the other debris. I clearly recall catching more fish during such periods

ROSE HIPS

and it may be that the cormorants know this too. Certainly, they're better fishermen than I ever was.

Young herons have to fend for themselves from now on, having been abandoned by their parents some weeks ago. I watched one youngster catch and try to swallow a sizeable eel along a ditch that feeds into the Severn. Catching it was obviously the easy part because, try as it might, the poor bird could not disentangle the struggling eel from around its neck and beak. As the eel clung on for dear life, the heron tried everything including shaking its head vigorously from side to side and clawing at the creature with its long toes. Eventually, the eel loosened its grip and made a break for the water – a fatal mistake. The heron stabbed it repeatedly around the head, picked it up in its beak and swallowed it in one fluid movement.

24th September I always find it fascinating to take a party of schoolchildren out into the country and watch their reaction. This morning, it was the turn of pupils from Ysgol Dafydd Llwyd and, after walking the few hundred yards from the school yard to the park in the middle of Newtown, we spent the next hour looking for seeds, leaves and old bird nests. I clearly remember doing this when I was in the primary school in Llanwddyn and it was comforting to note that the children of today are just as enthusiastic about their wildlife as I was when I was a lad.

Everyone had to have a conker to take back with them, so much of the time was spent searching the ground beneath the horse chestnuts, and they were all particularly fascinated by the creepy-crawlies that lived beneath the bark of a dead tree. The woodlice, spiders, slugs, beetles and ladybirds drew gasps of astonishment from an admiring audience; this was far better than maths or spelling in a stuffy school classroom. We only saw two species of birds, several carrion crows and a handful of woodpigeons, but we all had a wonderful time. It's so important that children are taken out into the countryside and shown the wonders of nature as they are the conservationists of the future. Most will not turn out to be wildlife enthusiasts but at least they'll appreciate the natural wealth that surrounds them.

September 26th At least once a month over the winter, I try to take the family to the west Wales coast. I love the summer sun but at that time of year, the beaches are too crowded for me and I much prefer to walk the shoreline on a stormy autumn or winter's day. Today we visited Ynys-las at the mouth of the Dyfi river.

There were few flowering plants amongst the dunes but a handful of meadow pipits had made their way down from the uplands to escape the worst of the weather. Small flocks of linnets hung like acrobats from the tops of teasel and carline thistles, their sharp beaks seeking out the seeds that lurked within. Rabbits had grazed much of the dune slack so that it looked like a well-manicured lawn and the last few wheatears were frantically trying to stock up their internal larder before heading off towards the arid landscape of the sub-Sahara.

Huge, brown fox moth caterpillars were everywhere, each one the size of a man's middle finger. They feed on a variety of food plants, depending on the habitat, but the ones at Ynys-las were feeding principally on brambles and, in the wetter areas, meadowsweet. This caterpillar will then overwinter beneath the moss layer before it pupates in a long, cigar-like cocoon. The adults are large, red-brown moths with two parallel, pale bands across the forewing and are active in early summer, the male flying in daylight.

Whilst visiting nearby Borth beach a few days earlier, I'd noticed thousands of blue, disc-like pieces of 'plastic', but in my ignorance, I'd believed them to be cargo spilled from a passing ship. This time, I looked a little more closely and, having consulted the warden at the information centre, found out that they were a kind of jellyfish known as 'by-the-wind-sailors'.

Apparently, millions have been washed ashore all around the Welsh coastline, carried here by the North Atlantic Drift. When alive, they resemble a flat, bluish oval float with an erect triangular sail that allows the animal to drift with the wind and tide. In the past, I've seen large jellyfish, brittlestars (a kind of long, thin starfish) and even fish such as mackerel washed ashore in their thousands but I can honestly say that this is the first time I've ever noticed these fascinating animals on our tidelines.

September 27th It's been a good breeding season for goldfinches this year and this afternoon, I watched a flock of 34 feeding amongst the weeds on an area of rough ground adjacent to a new housing estate.

Because of their beauty, wild goldfinches have been trapped and kept as cagebirds for centuries but, thankfully, this is now illegal. However, I can well-understand our ancestors' desire to cage such a magical bird and bring some of that beauty into their drab homes. Other finches, such as the chaffinch and linnet, were also caught, but it was the goldfinch with its blood-red cheeks and golden wingbars that was most highly prized. Brian Jones, a good friend from Llangamarch, reported having seen his first fieldfares of the year yesterday. These are large, blue-headed and brown-backed Scandinavian thrushes that move south-west to overwinter here in Britain. I generally hear their 'chack-chacking' calls as they migrate overhead at night but I've yet to hear them, or their close relatives, the redwings.

September 30th Driving back home over Mynydd Epynt, I was struck by the beauty of the autumn bracken. Its golds, yellows, browns and greens covered wide swathes of the uplands, bringing a variety of colours to an otherwise uniform green environment. Most landowners hate bracken and see it as an invasive plant that should be controlled wherever it occurs but in the past, it was highly valued.

It has been used as fuel and tinder and its ashes were formerly used as soap. Many country folk used the plant for packing and padding fragile goods in crates and it was universally used as bedding for cattle. Indeed, in some parts of Wales, I still see one or two farmers cutting bracken to put under their animals as it is a much cheaper alternative to straw.

There is an old Welsh saying which states 'gold under bracken, silver under gorse and famine under heather'. This refers to the fact that whereas the soil beneath heather is agriculturally poor, bracken generally grows on fertile soil and my father, who grew up on a farm in south Wales, remembers the family ploughing up patches of dense bracken to grow potatoes.

Today, I see bracken as a valued wildlife habitat. The bracken, hawthorn and rowan *ffridd*, so common in some parts of Wales, are one of the last refuges for birds such as the yellowhammer, tree pipit and linnet, as well as butterflies such as the very rare high brown fritillary. In winter, I have seen meadow pipits, thrushes and even chough searching for food amongst the dead plants and you can always be sure that you'll see a hovering kestrel in such areas.

When I took the dogs for their evening walk across the open fields at the back of the house under a full moon, two tawny owls were calling to each other across the valley.

HUNTING AND SPROOTING

'When I was growing up in mid Wales, mistletoe was something we bought at Christmas to adorn the house and to take to school for an excuse to kiss the beautiful girls who wouldn't touch you with a bargepole for the rest of the year.'

FUNGI AND MOSS (photo: Steve Phillipps)

October 1st I'm no expert on mushrooms and toadstools but I know how to eat them! Indeed, I have eaten well over a dozen species in my time and one of those is the shaggy ink-cap. And I saw some today when out collecting conkers with the boys.

This is a very common fungus on roadsides and grassland and is best eaten when it first appears and the gills underneath are still white. Tall, and with cylindrical caps covered in a shaggy cuticle, as it gets older, its gills and spores turn into a dark liquid which drips down onto the grass beneath and it is this liquid that was used as ink in the olden days, hence the name. Lawyer's wig is another common name for it because of the shaggy appearance of the white cap.

October 2nd The whole family migrated south today to visit good friends of ours who live by the banks of the Usk, a few miles south of Abergavenny. Steve Roberts is a fine field ornithologist and it is always a pleasure to spend time in his company. Every spring and summer, he monitors breeding goshawks, hobbies, barn owls, long-eared owls, honey buzzard, hawfinch and several other bird species.

We walked from his house along the river where Steve had put down corrugated-iron sheets on an area of bracken and young woodland. Beneath one, we found skin shed by a grass snake and beneath two others, we caught a couple of field voles. The kids were fascinated and I have to confess that I thoroughly enjoyed myself too. It's so important

SPARROWHAWK (photo: Steve Phillipps)

to keep that child-like fascination for wildlife and there is no better teacher than Steve Roberts.

Later in the day, we walked through a field of cut oilseed rape and watched a flock of 40 linnets fly in loose formation in search of seeds. This is an excellent crop for wildlife as it produces thousands of small seeds and because it is not ploughed until the spring, the seed-rich stubble remains untouched throughout the winter. As we walked back towards the house, a female sparrowhawk flew straight through the middle of the flock, its talons shooting out to catch a linnet that was a fraction of a second too slow. In nature, that's often the difference between life and death.

October 3rd The winds and rain came with a vengeance in the evening and I watched as the leaves were torn from the branches of the hawthorn and rowan trees on the hills above the village of Dolfor. This left a landscape of autumnal bracken slopes with scattered berry-laden trees with the occasional meadow pipit making short flights from one tuft of grass to another, afraid to fly too high in case it was carried away by the strong gusts. I enjoy walking in such weather when I'm waterproofed from top to toe because I know there's nobody else out there, just me and the elements.

October 4th Today was a red-letter day! Walking along the banks of the Severn with the dogs, I heard the unmistakable high-pitched squeak of an otter. I watched for over 20 minutes as two otters gradually worked

OTTER (photo: Steve Phillipps)

their way up river against the strong current. It had rained steadily all night and the water level was high, so the animals kept to the far bank, occasionally going ashore to avoid a particularly tricky section of river.

Both animals called constantly and on at least two occasions, they dived underwater and came back up with fish. Despite the fact that I was wearing a bright red coat, they were completely oblivious to my presence. In truth, their eyesight is not good but they do have excellent hearing, so I kept my movements to a minimum and followed slowly as they moved up river. They were two youngsters, kicked out by their mother and told to find their own way in the world, but not yet old enough to establish their own territories.

Otters are now widespread throughout most of Wales and are doing particularly well in mid Wales. Up until ten years ago, I had never seen an otter but since then, I have seen them on at least two occasions each year, generally in autumn and winter and usually when the water levels are high. The Severn has been particularly productive in favoured areas and incredibly, many of these are within spitting distance of housing estates. I'll bet that hundreds of people will walk within a few metres of those otters today, completely oblivious to their presence.

October 5th After picking the kids up from school, I decided to take them over to Powis Castle on the outskirts of Welshpool. Under some regal oak trees behind the castle itself, we stumbled across a small herd of fallow deer hinds under the watchful gaze of a huge stag. At this time of year, the males are rutting, a process by which the dominant males establish a harem and fight to keep all other males at antlers' length. This stag, with its thick neck, huge palmate antlers and beautiful chestnut coat with white spots, gave an occasional deep bellow as a young male appeared briefly on the horizon.

Fallow deer were introduced by the all-conquering Normans in the twelfth century as they were easier to confine within high-walled hunting parks than the larger red deer. From these initial collections, escaped individuals have become established throughout much of England and Wales although in Scotland, red and roe deer are far more common. The herd at Powis Castle is semi-domesticated and this gives us, the public, an excellent opportunity to watch these large animals at close quarters. Certainly, my boys loved the experience and later that evening, Spiderman and Dr Octopus were briefly forgotten as they became two fighting stags!

wild about the wild | hunting and sprooting

October 6th Whilst driving over the Brecon Beacons in strong winds, I passed within a few metres of a common buzzard that was hanging in the air above the roadside verge, its wings and tail quivering in the wind but its head perfectly still.

In Wales, we have become rather blasé about these birds of prey because they are so common. The mixture of scattered woodlands, uplands and sheep pasture is ideal for them and in some parts of the Welsh Marches, they reach densities as high as anywhere else in Britain. The individual I saw hanging in the wind was a fairly typical buzzard with its brown and cream mottled chest but I have seen several very dark birds and others that are so white, they resemble a gull. I have also noted some individuals that are conspicuously larger than the average buzzard and often this gives rise to claims that golden eagles are, once again, roaming the hills of Wales. If only. . .

October 7th If you drive around Llyn Efyrnwy in October, you can't fail to miss the pheasants that scurry out of the way of passing cars to the safety of adjacent fields and woodlands. Many don't make it and on one five-kilometre stretch today, I counted 11 fresh corpses. Pheasants were introduced to Britain by the Normans but it would be several centuries before they became a common sight in Wales as thousands were released by shooting estates. Now, small syndicates also release birds each year and it is one of our commonest birds in the autumn.

Personally, I am not against hunting per se, especially as thousands of acres of wildlife-rich woodland have been kept as cover for gamebirds such as pheasants. Without the shooting, these woods would undoubtedly have been cleared to make way for intensive farmland or coniferous forests. However, I do find it rather strange that half-tame birds, which often have to be kicked in the backside to make them airborne, are shot down in the name of sport. Still, this odd pastime does bring hundreds of thousands of pounds into the rural economy and provides a living in areas where it is badly needed.

Far more difficult for me to understand is the attitude of some gamekeepers who will go to extraordinary lengths to persecute certain birds of prey, such as sparrowhawk and goshawk, that prey on pheasants. Poisoning, trapping and shooting these birds is illegal and yet it still goes on in some areas. I'm actually very supportive of the gamekeeping profession as I firmly believe that, in our man-made landscape, some control over crows, squirrels and certain other pests is

essential for other wildlife to flourish. However, I absolutely condemn those who flout the law and in many parts of the country, I'm convinced that road casualties far outnumber the pheasants taken by birds of prey.

October 9th The wind was whistling in from the east this morning and brought with it vast numbers of fieldfares and redwings. Even before first light, I could hear the weak wheeze of the redwing as they flew overhead but it wasn't until mid-morning that I heard the first 'chack-chacking' calls of fieldfares on the hawthorns in the fields behind the house. Migratory birds like these often build up in huge flocks, waiting for the winds to blow in the right direction and in the spring, you often see huge influxes of swallows and house martins when the wind

Cock Pheasant

changes to blow from the south. As fieldfares and redwings are mainly Scandinavian visitors, a cold easterly wind is perfect for them.

Ringing records have shown that the fieldfares we see in Wales and western Britain are mainly birds that have bred in Norway and that Swedish and Finnish birds winter in south-east Britain and parts of western Europe. There are two distinct races of redwing, one that breeds in Iceland and the other in Scandinavia and Russia, and it is the latter that overwinters in Wales. There is also a small breeding population in the highlands of Scotland and I was stunned to see a pair nesting in a garden in Aviemore when filming in the area this spring.

I always think that winter has finally arrived when these migrants arrive and the bitterly cold easterly winds did nothing to allay my fears. There were hundreds of crisp, grey-brown sycamore leaves carpeting the footpath as I walked the dogs this morning and both the poplars and elder trees were looking noticeably bare. Indeed, some of the leaves were falling around me like snow, ripped from the branches by the sharp east wind, and it was only beneath the beech, with its full complement of leaves, that I was able to find some shelter. To combat the chill, I wore a fleece for the first time since the spring and the piping hot mug of tea I sipped on my return home was very welcome.

October 10th I killed my sixth rabbit of the autumn this morning. All six had been suffering from myxomatosis, a viral disease that was introduced from South America to France, and then to Britain, in the early 1950s. At that time, it was estimated that rabbits were causing £50 million damage to crops each year but myxomatosis killed around 96% of British rabbits in just a few years. Buzzard, stoat and fox populations declined as the numbers of their main prey crashed and all three had to turn to other small mammals for food.

Rabbits were introduced to Britain from the western Mediterranean during the twelfth century for their meat and fur and as they were originally caged using woven fence panels and ditches, many escaped to the wild. In Wales, several of the islands became important rabbit 'farms' as there were few natural predators and, over the centuries, rabbit meat became a much sought after delicacy. Rabbits increased rapidly from the middle of the nineteenth century onwards when increased crop production and the establishment of large estates where foxes, stoats and birds of prey were killed in their thousands, provided an ideal habitat for them. It continued like this until myxomatosis arrived in 1953.

Even now, this awful disease hits our rabbit populations in cycles. Numbers build up for ten years or so, then myxomatosis hits once again and the rabbits seem to disappear virtually overnight. It is transmitted by the rabbit flea and in its later stages, infected rabbits are blind and deaf, and totally unaware of their surroundings. It's an incredibly cruel death as they stumble around open fields and roads, easy targets for the predators and passing cars that will finally put them out of their misery.

October 11th An old stone cowshed still supported a breeding pair of swallows, the adults swooping in and out through a broken window to feed their newly fledged young. This is incredibly late as pairs usually finish breeding in early September at the latest, giving the adults and youngsters enough time to build up fat reserves before starting the long journey to South Africa and Namibia. Whether this pair and its three offspring will survive is dependent on the weather. A warm spell may ensure that there are enough flying insects around but I fear this cold, easterly wind will spell disaster for them.

October 12th As if the cold wasn't enough, a persistent drizzly rain crept in this morning and stayed for the remainder of the day. Never mind, a run along the canal soon cleared the cobwebs and I was pleased to see that Hissing Sid, Aberbechan's resident mute swan-cum-rottweiler, still had five large cygnets in tow. Mallards were also enjoying the wet weather and I saw more moorhen than I've seen for a long time. They have been declining steadily here in mid Wales since

SWALLOW NEST AND YOUNG

mink colonised the area but the last two years has seen better breeding success.

October 13th I spent a few hours this morning sprooting around the local hedgerows in search of old nests for a nature walk I was due to lead later in the day. I love the word 'sprooting'. Basically, it means searching high and low, under rocks and in hedges, for anything and everything. Really, it's an excuse to be a child once again and to marvel at the hundreds of woodlice packed together under the bark of a dead tree or snails crammed into a narrow crevice in a stone wall. This morning, however, I was sprooting for old nests.

The best time to look for them is during the winter months when all the leaves have fallen and nests are far more visible. It is also important, of course, that they are no longer in use during the winter although I never collect wren nests because these are sometimes used as roosting sites by birds and small mammals. After an hour, I'd managed to find the solid grass nest of a song thrush with its mud lining, the horse hair-lined nest of a dunnock and a neat lichen-covered moss cup made by a chaffinch.

When I arrived at Llanfair Caereinion School, I was amazed by the pupils' response. They were astounded by the birds' ability to weave such magic with only a beak as a tool. With two hands and a sizeable brain, I could not hope to match their masterpieces. I must confess that I, too, was pleasantly surprised, not only by their reaction, but also by their knowledge and understanding of the wildlife around them. I picked up several feathers, all of which were correctly identified, and the few birds we saw on the river Banwy were first spotted by the children, not by me. Oh to have the eyesight and unwavering enthusiasm of a ten-year-old child once more!

October 14th It's not every day that you come across a fox in the middle of the day. But that's exactly what happened in Dinas Mawddwy today. Wandering through a mixed woodland on the outskirts of the village, my dogs suddenly became interested in a thick patch of brambles and despite calling several times, they would not come to heel. Having retraced my steps, I joined them on the edge of the brambles and immediately scared out a big dog fox. At close range, they really are beautiful animals. His rusty coat and large, bushy tail were in perfect condition and despite the presence of the dogs, he was in no great hurry and simply ambled away up the hillside.

Foxes are never as big in real life as you expect them to be, and without the large tail, they wouldn't be much bigger than a small collie. They are the ultimate survivor, having been shot, poisoned, trapped and hunted by man for centuries, but they are still here despite all our worst efforts. Since the extinction of the wolf, lynx and bear, the fox is one of our biggest predators and it's always amazed me how this animal, above all others, brings out extreme and opposing views in people.

Having grown up in the country and lived here nearly all my life, I've seen and heard both sides of the fox-hunting debate. I have little time for the red-coated toffs who swig a few gins and hunt foxes for fun. Where I grew up, however, it was never like this and fox-hunting involved a few landowners who came together once in a while to hunt down 'problem' foxes that had been taking lambs. Whether all the dead lambs were, in fact, killed by foxes is debatable but I have seen lambs killed by these predators and it's not a pretty sight. I have also worked to protect rare breeding birds such as hen harriers and little terns, often to find adults and chicks taken by a fox at the last minute. When this happens, I completely understand the frustration of farmers who lose lambs.

There's no doubting the fact that it's a very complex issue and involves not only the ethical argument of fox-hunting itself, but also the class war

RED FOX (photo: Steve Phillipps)

and the town-versus-country debate. I am, and always will be, a countryman, but we all have to accept that with an increasing number of people living in our towns and cities, that's where the big decisions will be made in future.

October 15th Never believe a weatherman. It was supposed to be wet and miserable today with prolonged showers but instead, it turned out to be a cold but gloriously sunny autumn day. It was a wonderful day to be out with the dogs and to cap it all, a ghostly barn owl floated over our heads as we walked back home in the semi-darkness along the country lanes.

October 16th There's nothing I like better than to walk in the company of a knowledgeable, no-nonsense field naturalist and today, I had the privilege of rambling through the town of Welshpool and the adjacent grounds of Powis Castle with one of the best, Clive Faulkener, the conservation officer for the Montgomeryshire Wildlife Trust.

Clive pointed out the ancient trees that were planted all around the grounds some two to three hundred years ago. Indeed, one wonderful old oak tree was a nature reserve in itself, despite the fact that it had become completely hollow over the years. This was a magnificent specimen, well over 10 metres in circumference and probably almost a thousand years old. It's incredible to think that when it was a sapling, the world had never heard of William the Conqueror and parts of Wales were still frequented by beaver and wolves.

The tree had seen better days and many of its branches were rotten but this made it even more interesting for wildlife. A wonderful fungus called the beefsteak fungus poured out of the rotting wood like a cow's tongue and every nook and cranny supported insects and spiders. It's said that our native oaks support almost 500 different species of insects whereas the introduced Sitka spruce, now so familiar in the Welsh countryside, supports fewer than a dozen. Wouldn't it be wonderful to see several of our conservation organisations working together to create a huge native woodland somewhere in Wales? Just think of the benefits to both wildlife and people.

October 18th It's wonderful to see how wildlife can, at times, adapt quite quickly to live alongside man. Today, as I drove from west Wales along the M4 motorway near Port Talbot, my eyes were drawn to a cormorant perched on top of one of the lamp posts in the central reservation. I've seen kestrels, pigeons, gulls and crows doing this many times, and occasionally, a buzzard or two, but never before a cormorant.

The bird was using the best possible perch adjacent to a good fishing pond that happened to be adjacent to Wales's busiest road. The pond, at Baglan, is a well-known haunt for cormorants and it appears that at least four of them are now using the lamp posts to rest up and dry their feathers before continuing with the task of finding a meal. I'm sure many birdwatchers have almost come to grief along this stretch of motorway, glancing again at the dark shape perched high above the car to make sure their eyes are not playing tricks on them.

Further along the motorway, I called in at Parc Slip, a man-made reserve near Ton-du that is also the headquarters of the Wildlife Trust for South and West Wales. This wonderful area is a former opencast coal site that has been transformed to the benefit of wildlife. In spring, the fields are full of lapwings, skylarks and a variety of orchids and the old canal is a stronghold for the very rare water vole. It's also a wonderful place to get good views of fairly common birds such as mute swans, moorhens and even the normally elusive kingfisher.

October 21st A day of gale-force winds and heavy showers saw me filming in the mountains around Capel Curig and despite the weather, there was something bleakly magnificent about the scenery. On the way, I had to dodge flocks of redwings and fieldfares that were being thrown everywhere by the wind and had therefore decided to fly along roadside hedgerows in search of shelter. Imagine flying all the way from Scandinavia to find an abundance of fruits and berries only to be thrown around so badly, you can't actually land to feed on them!

Before coming across the flocks of wintering thrushes, the only other birds I'd seen were a few crows but near Cerrigydrudion, a lone red kite stood out against the dark, menacing skies. Unlike the frantic flight of the redwings, the kite was completely at ease in this wind, its eyes fixed on the ground searching for prey while its tail twisted and turned to combat the sudden gusts. This magnificent bird is a superb flier and uses strong winds to fly effortlessly across the landscape in search of food.

Over the past ten years, the Welsh population has increased dramatically and southern Snowdonia now supports a small, but successful population. So far, they have escaped the clutches of egg

wild about the wild | hunting and sprooting

OCTOBER

RED KITE

collectors, and local landowners have welcomed them with open arms. Some are now nesting in northern Gwynedd for the first time in 150 years, a far cry from the dark days of the early twentieth century when only a handful of birds survived in central Wales.

October 22nd If anything, today was worse than yesterday. The gales are continuing from the south-west and bringing with them persistent rain, so it's a perfect day for a visit to the Wildfowl and Wetlands Trust Centre at Penclacwydd near Llanelli. This is a great reserve because no matter what the weather, you know that you'll be able to see birds at close quarters. In the past, I've visited so many places where the birds have been small specks on the horizon and no matter how spectacular or rare the species, I've always felt cheated.

Penclacwydd has a large collection of waterfowl from all over the world, including exotic ducks, geese, swans and even flamingos. You can also see British ducks here and I know several wildlife photographers whose stunning close-ups of wild teal, wigeon and goosander, were actually taken at the Llanelli Wetlands Centre. Because it's surrounded by an electric fence and is full of ponds and ditches, it's also one of the best places in Wales to find water voles, a small mammal that has declined by over 90% in the past 15 years.

One of their huge successes has been the establishment of a nature reserve along the northern edge of the Burry Inlet, the mixture of saltmarsh and shallow ponds providing excellent habitat for a variety of breeding and wintering waders. It's also a wonderful place for little egrets, small white herons with black legs and yellow feet that have colonised Britain from the continent in recent years. At present, more

EGRETS (photo: Steve Phillipps)

than 190 individuals make their way from the estuary to roost in the centre each evening but in the past, over 250 have occasionally been recorded.

I also enjoy visiting Penclacwydd because it has a well-stocked bookshop and a café that serves excellent cakes. There's no better way to end a day's birdwatching than sitting down in the warmth to enjoy a strong cup of tea and a home-made sponge cake.

October 23rd Any more rain, and I'll be on the phone to Noah first thing tomorrow morning. A good friend who works for the Environment Agency told me that on some rivers, the high water levels have prompted the salmon to run a month earlier than usual. On the Severn, we usually see the first few jumping the weir below Newtown in late November with numbers gradually building up through early December.

Salmon migration is an incredible phenomenon and is yet another example of the miracle of nature. When the fish are smoults of between one and four years old, they leave our rivers and head out to feeding grounds in the open sea where they prey on small herrings, sand eels and crustaceans. Until fairly recently, the exact location of these feeding grounds was unknown but scientists now know that they gather in huge numbers in the north Atlantic, south of Iceland, where they remain for a year or two. They then return to their natal areas, navigating by the Earth's magnetic field and the stars as well as a chemical memory which allows the fish to smell its own river.

Throughout Britain, numbers have declined over the past 20 years. As a young lad, I remember watching dozens of salmon making their way up the Seiont to spawn, but now I get excited when I see two or three. The reasons for the decrease in numbers are complex and include overfishing in the estuaries and at sea, pollution, silting of the spawning grounds and changes in sea temperature. Huge efforts are now being made throughout the country to attempt to reverse the decline and I sincerely hope they succeed because the salmon is much more than just a fish, it's an important part of our heritage.

October 25th Two days of heavy rain have caused several rivers to burst their banks and one that floods every winter these days is the Severn. Despite the weather, I took the dogs along a section of the Offa's Dyke Path that crosses the Leighton Estate on the outskirts of

Welshpool, so that I could look down on the Severn valley. The view was spectacular with the hundreds of acres of flood water glistening in the autumn sun.

In the woodlands, I saw my first woodcock of the winter. Well-camouflaged, it is a gamebird superbly adapted for woodland life with its cryptic feathers blending in perfectly with a background of bracken and leaves and its broad, rounded wings allowing it to fly at great speeds through thick forests. It is about the size of a dove with a very long beak that it uses to probe wet ground in search of earthworms. Even in prolonged dry weather, woodcock can always find damp soil where they search for food and the two bulging eyes either side of the rounded head give it 360° visibility. It's virtually impossible to sneak up on a woodcock!

October 26th On my way home from Llanelli, I called by the Gelli-aur Country Park near Llandeilo, a great place to stop for a cup of tea and a slice of cake. Out of the café window, you'll see a variety of woodland birds such as nuthatches, tits and woodpeckers as well as over a dozen fallow deer feeding in the woodland clearings. Unlike the chestnut-coloured animals in Powis Castle, these are much darker and lack the clear white spots along the flanks but they are nonetheless the same species. If you're ever passing through Llandeilo heading towards Llanelli with half an hour to spare, it's well worth a visit.

October 27th The high winds of the past few days have stripped the leaves off most of our deciduous trees and the plentiful supply of berries on the hawthorn is now more obvious than ever. The hazelnuts and conkers are long gone, as are some of the birds' favoured berries such as the guelder-rose and elder. I found the remains of cherry seeds in an old nest amongst some brambles this morning, a sure sign that it had been used by a wood mouse.

The ash is a peculiar tree. It was one of the last to come into leaf this year and it's one of the first to be stripped bare. The seeds, however, continue to hang stubbornly like a bunch of keys and they will remain on the branch until late winter when the absence of leaves allows them to be carried unimpeded on the wind. The seeds themselves closely resemble those of the sycamore and, as a child, my brother and I would grab handfuls at a time and throw them high into the air to watch them spiral earthwards like mad helicopters.

October 28th Whilst driving to Cardiff over the Dolfor moors, I disturbed a flock of 12 golden plover, the first time I've seen these birds in Montgomeryshire for more than a decade. It was such a pleasant surprise to come across them that I was sorely tempted to try to follow the flock and forget about the days' work at the BBC but unfortunately, common sense prevailed and I continued my journey south.

Golden plover are rare breeding birds in Wales with probably fewer than 80 pairs on our uplands, the vast majority of these on the Elenydd, a barren moorland that extends from the Elan valley in the north as far as Abergwesyn in the south. In spring and summer, the male is a stunning bird with its golden back, black belly and dark cheeks but in winter, the colours become more muted. They are relatively small birds, not much bigger than a blackbird, with narrow, pointed wings that allow for a rapid flight.

In winter, our breeding birds probably don't move very far but they come down from the breeding moors to feed on pastureland that supports high densities of earthworms. Many of these are traditional sites and have been used for decades, often in association with lapwing. Certainly, the Dolfor hills do not support flocks of golden plover each winter and I would guess that the small flock I saw was probably on its way to more fertile feeding grounds in the lowlands.

In Wales, one of the best areas to see these birds is at Ginst Point in Carmarthenshire. Some of the wet inland fields are covered by thousands of golden plover and lapwing in winter, and on one memorable occasion, I counted over 12,000 birds. I usually come across them on recently ploughed fields along the Welsh-English border and as a general rule, the further east you travel, the more golden plover you find.

October 29th I enjoy doing wildlife programmes for the radio just as much as for the television and this morning, I drove down to Erwood near Builth Wells to interview Ray Woods of the Countryside Council for Wales. An extremely knowledgeable and articulate naturalist, his speciality is lichens and lower plants but, today, I wanted to interview him about mistletoe.

When I was growing up in mid Wales, mistletoe was something we bought at Christmas to adorn the house and to take to school for an excuse to kiss the beautiful girls who wouldn't touch you with a bargepole for the rest of the year. It was not a plant I saw growing in the wild until we travelled down the Welsh Marches through Herefordshire when I clearly recall seeing round bundles high up in the canopy of treeless poplars and apple trees. Today, it is still a plant of the border country and the area around Builth is about as far west as it ventures.

It's a parasitic plant whose 'roots' lie deep within the host plant, be it a poplar, hawthorn, oak or any one of a wide variety of other trees. Its association with Christmas goes back to pagan times when the druids believed that it had magical powers because it was unsullied by the dirty soil of the earth. The most valued mistletoe was that which grew on oak and, according to legend, this had to be harvested using a golden sickle in order to make the most of its powers. It was supposedly a plant that brought great fertility and this is the origin of our kissing under the mistletoe today.

October 31st Earlier this year, I found a common wasp nest under a rotting oak trunk but I hadn't dared go near because of the hundreds of aggressive insects flying to and fro. This morning, I was able to lift the trunk to look underneath and to my amazement, the nest is still in use although the wasps are far less mobile. The nest itself is about the size of a football and although the entrance is an old vole hole, the remainder of the chamber has been excavated by the wasps themselves. It's an amazing feat of engineering because all the work was carried out underground in the dark and I find it rather sad that all their hard work will now go to waste as the nest rots over the winter. If I have time, I'll try to extract the whole nest later in the year, when all the wasps have died.

Beneath the ash tree which has given our house, Tan yr Onnen, its name, I came across a beautiful pale fungus with brown markings on the cap. It's one of the larger parasol mushrooms, but because I'm not an expert on fungi, I'm not too sure whether it's edible or not. In cases like this, the best thing is to err on the side of caution so I left it where it was for the local slugs and mice to enjoy. Mind you, I've got that nagging feeling at the back of my mind that I've allowed a wonderful meal to go begging.

GUY FAWKES AND COSTA RICA

'It was the first really frosty morning of the winter and the nasturtiums in a neighbour's garden looked as though they'd had a very heavy night on the beer.'

SUNSET OVER THE PACIFIC AT RIO SERENA, COSTA RICA

November 1st I can't resist a good book! So, a meeting in Shrewsbury today was all the excuse I needed to dash across to a wonderful bookshop near Attingham Park that sells tens of thousands of wildlife titles. And with some exciting and exotic foreign expeditions looming, I needed guidebooks so that I could swot up!

November 2nd The run through the woods at Gregynog Hall this morning was like a scene from a film with leaves falling like snow all around me. It was absolutely stunning with the beautiful golden-orange leaves of beech and hazel falling in their thousands to carpet the path before me. In the more exposed areas, the trees were bare but in the sheltered valleys, several trees still had most of their leaves and a few large oaks looked out of place in their resplendent green.

November 3rd I don't make the journey to Aberystwyth very often these days but whenever I travel west to this lovely coastal town, I always enjoy my visit. Today, the autumn sun accompanied me as I drove along the A44, shafts of light occasionally picking out circling red kites and buzzards as we passed Nant-yr-arian, the kite-feeding centre. Last winter, two white kites were seen here but of the dozen birds I saw in passing, not one showed any aberrations in colour.

I walked the dogs along the banks of the Ystwyth which enters the sea on the southern edge of the town. The harbour supported its usual array of gulls and cormorants but it was on the steps of the breakwater that I found some more interesting birds, a flock of 18 purple sandpipers. These small waders are winter visitors to our rocky shores and they breed in the arctic tundra of Greenland, Iceland and Norway. Unlike other waders, they do not head for estuaries and sandy beaches but gather at traditional sites on rocky coastlines.

In the summer, they have a stunning dark purple plumage and although this has faded by the time they reach Wales, the colour is still very distinctive. The small group on the breakwater were sheltering from the crashing waves, no doubt waiting for the tide to ebb before heading back to their feeding grounds on the rocky beach near the old university.

November 4th The last of our summer migrants have long gone, with most of them flying south to the warmer climes of southern Africa. Today, however, I saw a chiff-chaff skulking amongst the bushes in the gardens of Bodelwyddan Castle near St Asaph in north-east Wales. At first, I wasn't too sure what the bird was because just as it came into view, it kept disappearing into the shrubs once more, constantly searching for insects. Once it came onto the outermost branches, however, it was unmistakable, diminutive and dull greenish-brown in colour.

November 6th Bonfire Night passed relatively quietly here in the village although the dogs spent most of the evening under the kitchen table. I often wonder what our wild animals make of all the explosions although I'm sure that plenty of hedgehogs, mice and voles are burned alive in the bonfires. At least it was a dry night and I hope everyone has now had their fill of fireworks so that my evening walks between now and the end of the month aren't accompanied by bangers and rockets.

November 7th A brisk run along the canal this morning brought me face to face with Hissing Sid, the mute swan's answer to George W. Bush. His motto is 'If it moves, attack it', and he lived up to his name again today. To be fair, he's only protecting his family (which is more than you can say for George W.), but it's an ever-decreasing family as he is now down to only four cygnets. At the beginning of the spring, his mate was sitting on at least seven eggs, six of which eventually hatched.

Fairly soon afterwards, one cygnet fell victim to a fox but I had high hopes for the remaining five as they had survived for several months along the same section of the canal. There does not appear to be any food shortage and it's quite natural for a brood to be whittled down over the course of the year. If these remaining four youngsters survive until next spring, they will have done well, but their survival may depend on the ferocity of the forthcoming winter. A mild winter and they should do well, but a prolonged cold period could spell disaster. No doubt they will be helped through these long, dark months by the good people of Aberbechan who daily throw out bread and cakes to the hungry family.

I took the children north to meet up with my parents and my sister's family, a journey that took me across Porthmadog cob. Built to keep the sea at bay, the landward side is an excellent area for a variety of ducks and wading birds and today, regimental rows of wigeon could be seen grazing the saltmarsh. The males are beautiful ducks with grey bodies, rusty heads and cream foreheads but the females are a drab brown and often difficult to distinguish from all the other female ducks.

Small numbers of wigeon breed in Britain but the Porthmadog birds are winter visitors from the far north. I stopped the car for a few minutes to listen to the far-carrying whistles of the males and I was immediately struck by how busy they were. Their feeding is governed not by daylight but by the tides. They can feed whilst the tide is out but they must rest or look elsewhere for food when the incoming tide covers the saltmarsh vegetation upon which they graze. At Porthmadog, the tide was receding and therefore the wigeon, along with a variety of other ducks and geese, were making the most of the newly-exposed plants.

November 8th On the way down to Cardiff, I stopped on the banks of the Usk near Brecon and was delighted to hear a dipper singing merrily from a boulder in the middle of the river. At a time when nearly all the other birds have fallen silent, it was wonderful to sit and listen to this small, plump bird singing at the top of its voice before flying downstream to chase away a rival.

Dippers hold a territory throughout the year and this must therefore be defended no matter what the weather. It's actually quite a tuneful song and I expect I'll hear much more of these little birds now that the winter is upon us as they'll be preparing to nest in early spring. Its territory must contain not only a suitable nest site but also enough prey to feed

DIPPER (photo: Steve Phillipps)

several beaks through spring and summer. The nest itself is like a ball of moss, often placed under a bridge or tucked out of the way in the bank, and birds are usually incubating eggs by early March.

In recent years, dippers have enjoyed mixed fortunes on Welsh rivers with acid rain and widely fluctuating water levels causing declines in some areas. On the whole, however, they appear to be holding their own and there's no better sight in early spring than two dippers, fat brown birds with bright white bellies, chasing each other down a clear upland stream.

November 9th I drove back from Cardiff in the dark, hoping to catch a glimpse of one of our more timid nocturnal animals. When I have enough time, I'll sometimes take a rather circuitous route along small country lanes in order to increase my chances of such an encounter. Tonight, the only foxes and badgers I saw were dead ones but I did have a close encounter with a dazzled hare.

Hares are now very scarce animals in Wales, mainly due to the shift from mixed to pastoral farming in western Britain, but I do sometimes come across them whilst travelling at night. This individual stood frozen in the middle of a narrow road that crosses one of the Radnorshire commons and at first, I thought that it had been injured. I was able to get out of my car and walk right up to it before it realised what I was and took off towards the cover of the bracken.

It's certainly the closest I've ever been to a live hare and it must have been temporarily blinded by my car headlights before realising the danger it was in and taking flight. At close range, the long back legs and huge ears are very obvious and I was quite taken aback at the speed with which it took off. It had covered half the hillside before I had time to get back in the car, zig-zagging through the tall vegetation with consumate ease.

Unfortunately, only a few hundred metres further along the road, I came across another hare that had recently been killed by a passing car. I wonder whether this was its mate? If so, I hope there are plenty of other hares around as the habitat appeared to be perfect for them and it would be wonderful to come back in the summer and see some leverets.

November 10th I had an hour to spare before doing a radio programme in north Wales so I took the dogs for a walk along the river. Once I'd left the noise of the local housing estate, I could hear a flock of redpolls 'chink-chinking' merrily as they flew along a line of alder trees growing along the banks of the Severn.

Redpolls are seed-eaters and you usually see them, as I did this morning, feeding in a tight flock amongst the branches of alder or birch trees. Using their pointed beaks, they tease the seeds from the small cones before moving on to the next tree to feed again. It's at this time of year that they are most confiding and I was able to get close enough to see the prominent red spot on the male's forehead without using binoculars.

Whilst watching these enchanting birds in the tops of the trees, I obviously wasn't paying enough attention to where I was putting my feet because I almost twisted my ankle on a golf ball that lay partially hidden amongst the grass tussocks. At first, I cursed the golfer whose drive along the course on the opposite side of the river had obviously gone astray, but then I remembered a golfer telling me that a small group of carrion crows had recently started to steal golf balls from the fairway. At first, it was only one bird that took the balls but it then brought its offspring along and soon, the habit spread.

Whether the crows are golf fans or not, nobody knows, but at least I'll know where to find a cheap supply of balls should I decide to take up the sport.

November 11th Today, I had the pleasure of visiting Coed Carmel National Nature Reserve near Llandeilo, an area of woodland, fields, bracken-covered slopes and a seasonal lake, all of which support a huge variety of wildlife. This morning, however, I was looking for signs of small mammals in the company of Andrew Lucas, a mammal expert from the Countryside Council for Wales.

Without trapping them, it's almost impossible to find mice and voles, therefore Andrew collects old hazelnuts to find out exactly what's been eating them. A nut that's been cracked in half has been opened by the strong jaws and teeth of a grey squirrel, and we found plenty of those. Mice and voles, however, gradually gnaw their way into the nut but each species does so in a different way. The bank vole gnaws a fairly rough, circular hole with no gnaw marks on the outside whereas the wood mouse leaves obvious gnaw marks around the outside of the hole. The rarer dormouse also leaves gnaw marks but its hole is a perfect circle, as if it has been opened by a can opener.

I don't remember seeing dormice or any of their signs when I was a young lad growing up in mid Wales, and they are more often seen in lowland deciduous woodland. These days, scientists are finding more of them as they search our woodlands and now that I know some of the signs to look out for, it'll be interesting to see whether there are any in my immediate vicinity. Some people also erect specialist nest boxes for this species, a box that has its small circular hole facing inwards towards the trunk. This makes it far easier to monitor the animals during the breeding season when they build circular nests in the boxes. Remember, however, that it is an offence to interfere with dormice or their nests unless you have a special licence.

November 12th It was a journey back in time for me today as I headed to Llanwddyn, the small village in the foothills of the Berwyn mountains where I grew up. It's a wonderful area with a wealth of wildlife and some great local characters and it's always a privilege to go back there. And although I saw precious little wildlife today, the view from the hills looking down along the lake was stunning. The dark green conifers contrasted wildly with the yellow-orange larch trees, and hazel, oak and beech provided a golden fringe for the dark grey waters of the lake. Most beautiful of all, however, were the red and brown, bracken-covered slopes that climbed steeply towards a blue, cloudless sky. I can't recall ever seeing it look more beautiful.

November 13th The first of two days as a guest lecturer in the Wildfowl and Wetlands Trust centre at Martin Mere in Lancashire, so an early start was called for. It was the first really frosty morning of the winter and the nasturtiums in a neighbour's garden looked as though they'd had a very heavy night on the beer.

Martin Mere is west of the M6 a few miles south of Preston and it lies in an area of fertile, arable land a few miles from Morecambe Bay. It is most famous for its wintering pink-footed geese and whooper swans although it also supports thousands of other wintering wildfowl and waders.

I was so mesmerised by the sheer volume and variety of birds before me that I was late for my lecture!

November 14th Rather than stay in the area overnight, I decided to drive home and travel back up to Martin Mere the following morning. Today, my lecture was in the afternoon so I took my time getting to the reserve and drove around some of the quiet country lanes in the surrounding flatlands.

I do wish we had more arable land in Wales. A monotone of overgrazed rye grass is good for nothing except sheep and crows and I strongly believe that Welsh agriculture is in for a fall sometime in the near future because we've got all our proverbial eggs in one pastoral basket. Around Burscough, some of the recently ploughed fields had small flocks of golden plover and lapwing walking around looking for invertebrate food and where pools of water still lay on the surface, teal and mallard were feeding around the edges.

I passed several arable fields that had been left fallow and these were crawling with small finches, including linnets and goldfinches. Kestrels and sparrowhawks were common, no doubt drawn in by the feast of smaller birds, and a lone fox crossed a field of turnips as it made its way towards a nearby copse. No doubt these fallow fields have been entered into an English agri-environment scheme whereby money is made available to the farmer to manage his land for the benefit of wildlife. Despite much attention in the press, I fear our own agri-environment schemes here in Wales are having very little positive effect on the countryside; certainly, I'm seeing fewer yellowhammers, lapwings and hares in the Welsh countryside now than I was almost 20 years ago when these schemes first appeared.

I left Martin Mere just as the last orange glow was disappearing over the horizon and as I drove away, I was met by wave after wave of pink-footed geese making their way back to the sanctuary of the reserve after feeding all day in the surrounding fields. It was a magical sight, like waves of fighter-bombers making their way back to base after a successful foray.

November 16th I was up at 4am this morning to walk the dogs around the fields before leaving for ten days' filming in Costa Rica via Heathrow. Every time I board an aeroplane, I'm very conscious of the fact that had God meant us to fly, he would have given us wings. Still, for ten days' filming wildlife in Costa Rica, I'd pilot the plane myself.

November 17th Having reached San José, the capital of Costa Rica, late last night, we set off (in a slightly less comfortable plane) towards the small town of Puerto Jimenez in the south-west of the country, where we met up with our guide, Mike Boston, before driving the 20 kilometres to Carati airport in a Landrover. Parts of the track had been washed away in recent floods but our driver was able to navigate around all obstacles as we drove through rainforest, fields and marshes to reach our destination. We stopped several times to film a variety of wildlife – scarlet macaws feeding on almond seeds, a beautifully-marked tiger heron fishing along a small stream and a strikingly-coloured king vulture with its bald, multicoloured head.

The most spectacular discovery was the very rare jaguarundi that crossed our path as we rounded a sharp bend but by the time we stopped, it had melted into the surrounding forest. Our guide was stunned as it was only the second time in eight years that he'd seen one of these short-legged, long-bodied big cats. Similar to the larger cougar, they are often active during daylight hours but nearly all sightings, like ours, are fleeting glimpses.

Carati airport turned out to be no more than a gravel path, just wide enough to accommodate a small, single-engined plane aboard which I was given a low-level tour of the rainforest canopy. It was absolutely stunning. Large blue morpho butterflies, black vultures and chestnut-mandibled toucans flew past the window and try as I might, I couldn't see a single square inch of the rainforest floor through the thick canopy. Strangling figs, creeping vines and a myriad of epiphytes could be seen fighting to reach the bright sunlight but from the air, I could only guess at the daily struggles of the wildlife down below.

Landing on a cleared area of grass no more than 150 metres in length was fun. The pilot rammed on his brakes and used the rudder to skid left and right, like trying successive handbrake turns in a car on a wet field. By all accounts, he's the only pilot in the whole of Costa Rica who can do this. The others are probably all dead!

November 18th An early morning start from our base at the Sirena Biological Station in the Corcovado National Park saw us follow the trails through the rain-forest. The humidity and the incredible noises hit you soon after daybreak and as the light increased, we began to make out the tracks of several animals that had walked the same path during the night.

One of the animals that crossed the track in front of us (before leisurely climbing up one of the tallest trees I've ever seen) was a tamandua or lesser anteater. It is largely arboreal and feeds on termites, using its large front claws to dig these insects out of their concrete mud nests. This individual proved to be an ideal subject to film as it casually walked from branch to branch before returning to the ground to continue its journey. About the size of a raccoon, it has a long tail and long nose with a tan-coloured front and dark back but the sight of its long claws should be enough to warn any potential predator to keep its distance.

Overhead, several species of monkey could be heard, and occasionally seen, moving and feeding in the canopy layer. Red-backed squirrel monkeys are small, agile creatures that feed mainly on insects which they find on leaves and small branches whereas the much larger mantled howler monkeys feed principally on leaves. The latter are lazy animals which lie along branches for most of the day, picking at the occasional leaf and periodically joining in a chorus of unearthly howls which gives the species its common name. They are most vocal at dawn and anyone visiting the national park in the future shouldn't worry about bringing along an alarm clock as you will be awoken at precisely 4.45 every morning by the mantled howler monkey male-voice choir.

Our base, Sirena Biological Station, is a series of interconnected wooden huts that are used by research students and hikers and, for a small fee,

TAPIR

wild about the wild | guy fawkes and costa rica

you can add three basic meals to the price of your basic accommodation. The food is good and there's plenty of it, as long as you like rice and beans three times a day.

November 19th A short walk through the forest brought us to the mouth of the river Sirena, where the nutrient-rich freshwater reaches the sea. On the far shore, a huge crocodile, over four metres in length, lay basking in the warm sunshine and, periodically, we saw the menacing shapes of bull sharks patrolling the fish-rich waters. We had been warned not to swim here; now, I saw why. Pure white snowy egrets and small blue herons waded through the shallows looking for fish and frogs but each one kept a wary eye out for passing crocs.

Whilst walking a trail no more than a hundred metres from the estuary, Mike's sharp eyes spotted a tapir wallowing in some deep mud in the forest. How he'd seen it, I do not know because the animal was motionless and blended in perfectly with the surrounding vegetation. Tapirs, or Baird's tapir to give this one its proper name, are common in this part of Costa Rica and a long-term study has been undertaken to improve our understanding of their habitat requirements and movements. This animal was obviously part of that study because when it finally got up out of the mud, we could see its radio collar, an electronic device which emits a silent signal so that it can be followed by the scientists.

It showed no fear and ambled gradually away from us, eating as it went. They are unable to climb and therefore rely on the leaves and fruits that grow within a metre and a half of the ground. They are particularly fond of wet areas and we were able to watch as its large, three-toed feet allowed it to walk over the swampy surface with ease. The tapir was one of the South American animals that I'd always wanted to see and having failed to find them on two previous trips, this was to be a day that I would always remember.

Our tactics were to get up and film before dawn, take a break through the middle of the day when most animals take a siesta, and work again until last light. Today, however, was different as we were challenged by the locals to a game of football on a pitch that can best be described as a paddy field. Despite using all my rugby training, we lost to a highly disputed goal but it must be said that the Costa Ricans, like the Brazilians, are born with a football glued to their feet.

November 20th It wasn't the howler monkeys that woke us this morning from our wooden-slatted bunks but an earthquake that measured 6.4 on the Richter scale. Later, we were to learn that it had caused mudslides throughout the south-west of the country and that four people had died, three of them from heart attacks.

We climbed up through the forest to some of the low-lying hills above the coastal plains. En route, I caught a small barred racing snake, a superbly well-camouflaged snake with huge eyes that hunts lizards and large insects among the leaf litter. I love snakes but I won't handle them unless I know exactly what they are. I learned my lesson the hard way a few years ago when I tried to pick up a 'harmless' snake that turned out to be a cobra! Never again.

As we approached a group of coconut trees, I could hear an odd ripping sound and on closer inspection, we found a red-tailed squirrel gnawing its way into a coconut. Similar in size and colour to our own red squirrel, it was working hard to get at the white flesh when it was chased away by the much bigger coati, the largest and most conspicuous member of the raccoon family in Costa Rica. This individual then feasted for over an hour on its ill-gained meal before retreating into the forest, no doubt as full as an egg. We were about to dismantle the camera and move on when the squirrel re-emerged and began to feast on the now easily-accessible coconut meat. I wonder

COATI

COSTA RICAN BATS

whether it was secretly pleased that the coati had come along and done the hard work for it?

November 21st This morning, we walked to Rio Sirena's sister river, the Rio Claro. This is a much safer waterway as it does not have crocodiles or bull sharks, merely a few caimans. These are South American alligators which grow to no more than two metres in length and therefore pose no threat whatsoever to mankind. They are hugely adaptable and take advantage of virtually any open water, from rivers and streams to lakes, ponds and even water troughs.

The heliconia is a plant that will be familiar to many gardeners and out in Costa Rica, it is particularly common along the damp riverside soils. One species of bat, Spix's disc-winged bat, makes its home in the tube-like emerging leaves of this plant and uses sucker-like discs on its wings so that it can hang on to the inside of the leaf as it roosts. It is one of the few bats to roost upright as the vast majority, like all the British species, roost upside down.

About two kilometres up the Rio Claro, we found a deep pool and decided to dive in for a swim. I can honestly say that despite several daily cold showers, this was the first time during the whole trip that I had felt cool. The river water was so refreshing, we all felt vaguely human once more.

Whilst drying out on the shingle bank, we were able to film several large and colourful butterflies and a white hawk, one of the most stunning birds of prey I've ever seen. Its body is almost completely white apart from some black on the wings and a black band across the tail. It glides through the canopy like a phantom in search of snakes, lizards and frogs and nests amongst the uppermost branches of the tallest trees.

We were on the verge of leaving when Mike, our ever-dependable guide, saw a family of southern river otters playing on the far side of the river. Like our own European otter, they are shy animals but because we were in the shadows of some fallen trees, we were able to film the mother and two well-grown cubs for more than ten minutes. During that time, she emerged from the water on several occasions and twice, she fed on freshwater crayfish on the far bank. It was a memorable sighting and the perfect end to an excellent day.

November 22nd Much of the morning was spent packing damp clothes into damp rucksacks and frantically looking for passports that had been cast aside a week earlier. Before our flight back to London, there was just enough time for a revenge football match and, given the much drier conditions, I was convinced that we could gain revenge. The result was Costa Rica 1, Wales 3 and we'd salvaged some pride with three cracking goals.

I was sad to leave the lowland rain-forest of the Corcovado National Park with its incredible wealth of wildlife and welcoming rangers but a cold beer awaited our return in Puerto Jimenez and after a week without a proper bed or dry clothes, a cold beer is a very tempting proposition.

wild about the wild | guy fawkes and costa rica

As it turns out, one cold beer became a dozen or more as we said farewell in style to our inimitable guide.

The following day-and-a-half was spent retracing our steps to Heathrow via San José and Washington with just enough time en route to fall out with a surly (and very short) customs officer in Washington Dulles airport. I don't know what it is about the Americans but they have the most miserable customs officers on Earth and they could certainly learn a lesson or two from the Costa Ricans.

November 24th A lovely crisp winter's morning gave me the opportunity to walk some of the lanes around the village for the first time in nearly two weeks. I found the familiarity of my local patch comforting and although I loved the visit to Costa Rica, it's always nice to come home to the family.

The most obvious difference from when I'd last walked this way was the distinct lack of leaves on any of the trees. When I left, a few stubborn oaks still clung on to their light brown blanket but now, all but a few had been ripped away by the autumn winds leaving bare branches all around. Muck had been spread on many of the surrounding fields and

WHOOPER SWANS (photo: Steve Phillipps)

this had attracted a variety of rooks, starlings, fieldfares and even a few lapwing. The dogs disturbed a nest of wood mice under a pile of logs near the house but having reinforced the pile and added a mixture of dry leaves and grass, I'm confident they'll be able to use their home again over the winter.

November 26th The whooper swans are back on the fields below the village of Aberhafesb, a few miles up the river Severn from Newtown. They return to the same few fields year after year and although they sometimes disappear to the upland lakes nearby for a few days at a time, these lowland fields are their favoured feeding areas. I wasn't able to pull over to count the birds properly but there were at least 14, six of which were juveniles. Last year, I counted a maximum of 31 whooper swans at the same site with only six juveniles. The latter are easily distinguished by their muddy-grey plumage and colourless beaks whereas the adults have a striking white plumage and an obvious yellow wedge on their beaks.

I'll keep an eye on this area over the forthcoming weeks as numbers should build up again but I'm very heartened by the numbers of youngsters because it signifies that the birds have had a successful breeding season in Iceland. Generally, only about 20% of the birds are juveniles, therefore a figure of almost 50% is very good news and bodes well for the future of this flock.

The fields where the swans overwinter are, in mid-Wales terms, huge. This is ideal for the birds because they have good all-round visibility while they graze, keeping a wary eye out for their only natural predator, the fox. Disturbance isn't a big issue as the farmer leaves them alone, apart from the few occasions when he needs to gain access to the field with his tractor but even then, the birds appear to have become accustomed to the landowner and his machinery. Whenever I pull over in my car to count the swans, they become instantly alert and waddle slowly down towards the river's edge but rarely do they take flight, probably because it uses up so much energy.

November 27th Yet another crisp morning with clear skies and frost carpeting the fields and hedges. Even the rooks were quiet as I went into Newtown to participate in my weekly radio programme but there was no stopping the few robins that sang bravely beneath the street lights.

Later in the day, I had to take part in a Welsh football programme at

MINK (photo: Steve Phillipps)

Caersws, a small village on the river Severn. The game itself, between Caersws and Bangor, was interesting enough but, towards the end of the game, my eye couldn't help being drawn back towards the bank of the river where a skulking black shape that I initially believed to be a moorhen, turned out to be a mink. These voracious North American predators are now common throughout most of southern Britain and some individuals are remarkably bold, taking very little notice of people. I remember walking the river Teifi in 1990 and having two mink run right past me, one chasing the other. I'm pleased to say that over the past few years, I'm seeing more otters and fewer mink than I used to, hopefully a sign that the latter is declining as the otter population recovers.

November 28th My first run since returning from Costa Rica took me along the frozen, leafy paths of Gregynog Hall. The pond was alive with birdlife, a mixed flock of teal and mallard vying for position with the resident moorhen and kingfisher. I never see teal or kingfisher here in summer but once the first frosts appear, they become regular visitors. It's a shallow pond, full of invertebrates, with plenty of cover and is therefore ideal for both of these species. Whereas the teal tend to hide away amongst the reeds, venturing out only briefly to feed, the kingfisher sits on overhanging branches waiting for an unwary fish to pass beneath him.

November 30th The male goosanders are back on the Severn. These are beautiful birds, far more dramatic than the drab grey-brown females, with their dark green heads, bright red beaks and white bodies. Since mating in March and April, they have spent several months moulting their feathers in the large fjords of northern Norway. It has been estimated that about 35,000 male goosanders from western Europe gather in this remote area before returning to their breeding grounds in late autumn. I have seen males returning to some Welsh rivers and lakes in October but they come back to the river Severn around Newtown in mid-November, adding some colour to an otherwise drab winter scene.

I saw my first lesser spotted woodpecker for many months this morning as I walked along the canal near Abermiwl. It was within a few hundred metres to where a pair had nested in a dying alder earlier in the year and I hope this is an encouraging sign for next spring because the number of pairs I see in the area has declined gradually from four to only one over the past six years.

Lesser spotted woodpeckers are easily distinguished from the great spotted by their small size – no bigger than a sparrow – and the lack of an obvious white shoulder patch. In spring, they are much more vocal and their drumming can be heard for quite a distance on a still morning, although getting a good view of one is not easy. Around Newtown, I generally find pairs nesting in alder along the banks of the Severn or the Montgomeryshire Canal although other pairs also nest in nearby deciduous woodlands.

TAIWAN AND LLYN TEGID

'I know of at least half a dozen birdwatchers that have visited Taiwan and failed to see either of these two species, so for us to come across both together was something quite special.'

DAWN, TU SHAN MOUNTAINS, TAIWAN

December 1st Where have all the wood mice gone? And the bank voles too? Well, who better to ask than another of Wales's excellent naturalists, Duncan Brown. He works for the Countryside Council for Wales and is a mine of information on Welsh mammals and their history. And so it was that I found myself bound for Abergwyngregyn near Bangor early this morning to interview him about a survey of small mammals that's been undertaken biannually at Aber National Nature Reserve (NNR) since the 1980s.

The crashing in the numbers of wood mice and bank voles has caused some consternation amongst the scientists. Generally, wood mice numbers are at their highest in late autumn following a long breeding season but this morning, not a single small mammal was caught. This is rather mysterious because we've experienced yet another mild winter followed by a very productive summer and autumn in terms of seeds, fruits and berries. Acorns, one of the wood mouse's chief food items, have been plentiful and yet the animals themselves appear to be very scarce.

This could have interesting consequences for several species of animals and birds that prey on small mammals. If there aren't enough mice, tawny owls will not breed at all in spring and a lack of small mammals can also affect foxes, kestrels and weasels. Interestingly, Duncan remarked that it had been a poor breeding season for pied flycatchers in Aber's many nest boxes as several of the nests had been predated by weasels. He wondered whether the weasel was forced to search out alternative prey because of the shortage of mice and voles. One of the wonderful things about wildlife is that there are always new discoveries to be made.

December 4th Despite the mild weather there are plenty of birds on the move and at 9.30 this morning, a huge flock of over 2,000 fieldfares and redwing passed over the house. They were heading west, with a few starling in tow, and no sooner had they disappeared from sight than a flock of 42 lapwing passed over in the opposite direction. These, I'm sure, had been attracted to the valley by a large ploughed field nearby but it was wonderful to see these enigmatic birds so close to home. Unfortunately, they are almost certainly continental birds spending the winter in Britain and come spring, they will wing their way east once more.

Having failed to find a single mouse or vole in Aber NNR a few days earlier, I disturbed four wood mice beneath a rotting log in the fields at the back of the house this afternoon. I was looking for, and found, hibernating toads, but the mice were a very pleasant surprise. I had also hoped to collect the old common wasp nest that I'd found a few months ago but this had rotted away to virtually nothing leaving a large cavity that provided a home for good numbers of woodlice and centipedes. I find the life beneath a rotting log or large rock fascinating and these days, with a good book, you can easily identify virtually everything you find.

December 6th I do like buzzards! They are by far the commonest bird of prey in Wales and it's wonderful to see them either soaring up above or perched on a roadside telegraph post looking for prey. This morning, I watched a well-marked individual being endlessly harassed by three carrion crows and no matter how high the buzzard climbed, the crows were never more than a few metres behind.

LAPWING (photo: Steve Phillipps)

I've always been amazed by the buzzard's patience; after all, it is a bigger and more powerful bird than the crow and yet it invariably heads off without retaliating. Crows mob buzzards and other large birds of prey because the raptors will take nestling and newly fledged corvids. Indeed, I've seen goshawks take fully-grown magpies and crows on several occasions. A crow is quite a large bird with a strong beak and therefore any potential predator has to carry out a pretty shrewd risk assessment before attacking one! After all, a bird of prey with a badly injured eye is a dead bird of prey. Only once have I seen a buzzard strike back, however, and that was in most spectacular fashion.

On that occasion, the buzzard was soaring near its nest as two crows came hell for leather out of a nearby copse. At first, the buzzard began to gain height in an attempt to escape but one crow flew above it and repeatedly pecked the feathers along its rump. Try as it might, the buzzard could not escape so it flipped over onto its back and a dazzling yellow talon shot out. Immediately, the crow fell earthwards like a black stone and, with a loud thud, hit the ground no more than 50 metres from my feet. When I approached the prostrate crow, I found that the buzzard's talon had opened its stomach like a surgeon's scalpel and the bird died, within minutes, in front of my eyes. The moral of the story? Crows shouldn't mob a buzzard having a bad day!

December 7th Today, a 15-hour flight awaits me as I leave for 11 days' filming wildlife on the island of Taiwan off the coast of China. I'm more excited about this trip than most because I know precious little about the place. I've looked around for books and identification guides, always a good move before visiting a new country, but at present, there are no guides specific to Taiwan. Never mind, I'm told that we have an excellent guide who speaks English and Mandarin so I'm sure we'll be in good hands.

The red kites were above the M40 near Oxford – just as they were before I left for Costa Rica. I wonder how many traffic accidents these birds cause as they distract the driver's eyes skywards? Certainly, when I saw one here for the first time some 15 years ago, I nearly hit the central barrier! It was also great to see so many kestrels hunting along the motorway embankments as this is a bird I don't see very often in Wales nowadays. As a young lad, I found two nests every spring within a kilometre of our house and the windhover, as it is also known, has always been one of my father's favourite birds.

wild about the wild | taiwan and llyn tegid

December 9th We finally arrived at our hotel in the north of Taiwan after a 33-hour journey via Amsterdam, Bangkok and Taipei.

This morning, we were up at 4.30, after 5 hours' sleep, to visit the Fu Shang National Park in the north-east of the island that was once called Formosa – the beautiful island – by the Portuguese. Fu Shang turned out to be a mist-covered forest with the occasional clearing and a small lake which attracted dabchicks and the incredibly beautiful mandarin duck. In Britain, mandarins have escaped into the wild from captive collections but they originate from the Far East. The female is typically a drab grey-brown colour. The male, however, is undoubtedly one of the most stunning birds in the world and my description of its amazing array of colours would not start to do it justice.

Another familiar sight was the muntjac deer that greeted us as we walked along the path towards the lake. No bigger than an average-sized dog, muntjacs are another of the endless list of plants and animals that have been introduced to Britain, and today they are flourishing in southern England and several have been seen along the Welsh border. In

MALE MANDARIN DUCK

time, I'm sure they'll become a familiar, if rather shy, visitor to woodlands, parks and gardens all over Wales.

These few species apart, the woodlands of Fu Shang were surprisingly quiet although the cool temperatures and the very Welsh rain may have been contributory factors. Begrudgingly, we moved south to Taroko Gorge National Park, although a landslide that had carried part of the main road with it, resulted in our arriving several hours later than planned.

December 10th After a glorious night's sleep in what had seemed unpromisingly sparse accommodation, I woke up full of the joys of a sunny Taiwanese winter's morning. The view out of the shack window was breathtaking. 600-metre cliffs extended upwards almost as far as the eye could see and far below was the raging torrent that had carved natural sculptures out of solid rock.

I tried, in vain, to squeeze my six-foot-one frame into a three-foot bath and eventually settled for a cold shower before heading down the gorge in search of wildlife. Up above, grey-faced buzzards and crested goshawks used the breezes rising from the sheer cliffs to circle skywards, and down by the river, a blue rock thrush was sunning itself by fanning out its wings and tail to catch the few rays that made their way to the bottom of the gorge.

Two species of redstart, the Daurian and plumbeous water redstart were very active, flitting in and out of the rocks in search of insect prey. The former is very similar to our own redstart but the males have a flash of white on the wings and the latter resembles a black redstart with a copper-brown tail and bottom. Far more drab were the brown dippers that flew inches above the raging waters, much as our own dipper does on the Welsh streams, and the constant cawing of the jungle crows added a reminder of home to the proceedings.

After dark, we moved on to a farm in the lowlands of the east coast, a few miles below the Tropic of Cancer. In the space of a few miles, we had moved from a temperate to a tropical zone. Let's hope this encourages the wildlife to be a little more co-operative.

December 11th Mr Lai, the owner of our fruit-farm home for the next two days, turned out to be an excellent naturalist and guide. He was also an enlightened farmer, accepting the fact that he would lose 40% of his crop to wildlife in return for the income created by visiting birdwatchers. He also refused to use chemical sprays on the twelve acres where he grew fourteen different kinds of fruit, including at least three that I had never eaten before in my life.

His farm turned out to be a magnet for birds, the ripe mangoes attracting the stunning Taiwan blue magpie, the island's national bird, with its bright red beak, black head, blue body and long blue tail. Unlike our magpie at home, it has become a scarce species in Taiwan and is now encouraged wherever it is found. Indeed, Mr Lai considered the fact that a group of seven magpies had set up home on his farm to be a good omen for the forthcoming harvest.

One of the most abundant creatures on the farm was a huge black and yellow spider that constructed large, round webs amongst the leaves of the banana trees. Called the human-face spider because of the shape on its thorax, it is non-poisonous although it does have quite a nasty bite when provoked. Believe me, when a spider the size of a man's hand is inches away from your face, the last thing you want to do is provoke it.

In the late evening, we were serenaded by several green tree frogs that had gathered at a small pond to prepare for the breeding season. By day,

HUMAN-FACE SPIDER

some individuals could be found glued onto any large leaf within jumping distance of the water so that the mating ritual could start again the following evening with minimal effort. At my age, I know just how they feel . . .

December 12th I was awoken at 5am by crowing cockerels – more fitting than a buzzing alarm clock, no doubt! A few metres outside my window, a Muller's barbet (a sort of green thrush-like bird with bright blue, yellow and red head markings) and a Taiwan babbler were busy tearing into the flesh of beetle nuts, an addictive national delicacy. Watching these birds feed, I could see how Mr Lai could lose almost half of his crop to the wildlife and I wondered how many farmers home in Wales would be quite so tolerant.

Having moved on to the southern tip of the island in the afternoon, we stayed the night in what appeared to be an army barracks high up in the mountains at Maulin. I'm sure there must be some luxurious hotels in Taiwan, but they seem to be avoiding us! Up until now the meals had, however, been varied and very tasty, with a healthy bias towards seafood. But not here. Breakfast was cold, wet rice with heavily salted duck eggs, a brown sludge that claimed to be seaweed and what I can only describe as grey mould – much the tastiest of the morsels on offer.

GREEN TREE FROG

December 13th A few hundred metres down the road from the 'hotel', we stopped at a small, heavily wooded tributary valley where millions of euploia butterflies gather to spend the winter months; the second largest gathering of butterflies in the world (after the monarch butterflies in Mexico).

As we walked up valley, butterflies hung like ripe fruit from the branches, leaves and tree trunks, but as the first rays of the sun broke the horizon, they suddenly began to flutter all around us like huge snowflakes in a blizzard of purple and blue. Such sublime moments of beauty remain with you forever.

Heading towards the coast allowed us our first look at the Taiwanese lowlands with their paddy-fields full of egrets, coconut groves and endless towns and cities. In the past 25 years, the island's population has tripled to 23 million and in order to accommodate all these people, the lowland forests and wetlands have disappeared. Our next target, the Tzengueu estuary, was an oasis in the middle of this urban desert and it provided a home for one of the rarest wetland birds in the world.

Black-faced spoonbills are delightful birds with their bright white plumage (in summer, they acquire some yellow 'bits'), black face and

EUPLOIA BUTTERFLY

long, spoon-like bills. They breed on a few islands off the coast of Korea and winter at two sites in Hong Kong and Taiwan. In the shallow waters of the Tzengueu estuary, we were looking at 700 spoonbills, over half the world's population of 1,200 individuals. It was at once exciting and extremely tragic to think that I could see the bulk of the world's population of one species through my binoculars.

December 14th Last night, we drove along one of the most tortuous routes in the world to reach the high Ali Shan mountains – and I mean high! The tallest mountain in Taiwan, Yu Shan, is 3,952 metres in height (over 12,000 feet). We drove up to 2,000 metres along some very narrow and dangerous roads that, in places, had been partially washed away by mudslides. I can only thank the heavens that we made the journey at night!

After another breakfast of wet rice and sludge, we walked through a plantation pine forest where the distant hammering of a woodpecker turned out to be a nutcracker using its strong beak to get at the seeds in a pine cone. There was no subtlety involved, just brute force, as it hammered the cone into submission before eating the seeds inside. A member of the crow family, the nutcracker is a common species worldwide but it has only been recorded eight times in Wales, most recently near Beddgelert in 1968.

Now came the time to descend the winding mountain roads. But this time in daylight! To make matters worse, no sooner had we reached the valley floor than we were climbing once more and aiming (by nightfall) for a hotel situated precariously on the upper slopes of one of the mountains at a height of just under 2,800 metres. Suffice it to say that, come bedtime, I felt compelled to use the electric blanket – the first time I've ever done this anywhere in the world!

December 15th The breakfast at this wonderful, family-run hotel was outstanding and we left at first light with our bellies filled to the brim. Immediately below the hotel was an area of pine woodland and scrub which attracted a good variety of birds. We filmed coal tits that looked like crested tits and called like great tits and we filmed green-backed tits that looked exactly like our great tits! All very confusing.

Later that morning, we climbed to the highest pass in Taiwan (3,158 metres) where laughing thrushes, with their brown and orange plumage, were scavenging amongst the rubbish dumped by hundreds

ALPINE ACCENTOR

of tourists. Even here, the hand of man had ruined the natural scenery. Alpine accentors, a mountain version of the dunnock, scraped a living amongst the higher outcrops of rock although they too could be persuaded to approach the tourist buses by the provision of bread and biscuits. I'd always wanted to see one of these birds ever since I'd read about the only Welsh record of an individual on the slopes of Snowdon in 1870. However, I wish I'd been able to see them away from the tourist buses and their rubbish.

Late afternoon saw us walking through an area of natural woodland further down the mountain in search of two of Taiwan's endemic birds, the dark blue mikado pheasant and the blue and white Swinhoe's pheasant, named after the nineteenth-century diplomat and naturalist, Robert Swinhoe. This was our last evening in the country and our last chance to find these shyest of species, so we all had our fingers and toes well-crossed as dusk approached.

Remarkably, we saw both species together as a small group of four birds crossed the path a few metres in front of us. First across was the splendid male mikado, a Japanese name which means 'emperor', and he was soon followed by two rather dull brown females. We had barely overcome the shock of actually finding these birds when a wonderful male Swinhoe's pheasant followed the party of three across the path, its long white tail feathers standing out in the dark wood.

I know of at least half a dozen birdwatchers that have visited Taiwan and failed to see either of these two species, so for us to come across both together was something quite special. We moved on to our hotel near Taipei in fine spirits although a late arrival in the city curtailed the celebrations somewhat.

December 19th 36 hours (and one evening in Cardiff) after leaving Taipei, I'm home! To get my body back into British time, I decided to go for a run along the canal with the dogs in the afternoon, a decision that was rewarded with the sighting of three kingfishers, all gathered to feed along a shallow section of water where the fishing was easier. Having extolled the virtues of male bullfinches, jays and barn owls in the past, I must say that with its vivid blues, greens and oranges, there's no beating the good old European kingfisher.

Later in the afternoon, I witnessed something quite extraordinary. Whilst enjoying a cup of tea on the front lawn, I watched a grey squirrel scurrying through a tall hawthorn hedge. It appeared to be in a great hurry although I could not see another animal in pursuit nor could I see a mammal or bird being chased. Suddenly, it gave an almighty leap into an adjacent hazel and landed on the back of a male blackbird. Despite the bird's frantic attempts to get away, it was killed instantly by the squirrel and taken out of my view, presumably to be eaten.

In the past, I have seen squirrels taking eggs and nestlings but never before have I seen them catching fully grown birds or, for that matter, hunting a bird with such rapidity. There has been much recent speculation about the role played by grey squirrels in the decline of many of our woodland birds and although one such incident does not make the squirrel public enemy number one, it does make you think.

December 21st Today, the shortest day of the year, saw my first visit to the town of Bala in several months. I always like travelling to this part of north Wales because it has so much to offer in terms of wildlife and scenery. For a start, I have to cross my favourite haunt, the Berwyn moors, to reach the town but there are also so many excellent walks around Bala.

In the town itself, there was something of a stand-off between the resident jackdaws and marauding herring gulls. The gulls, I assume, were using the adjacent Llyn Tegid as a safe roosting site, visiting the town itself in search of food. The jackdaws were obviously taking exception to these new immigrants and both species were shouting at each other from the rooftops when I arrived. Unfortunately, I wasn't able to observe the outcome as I had to move on to record a radio programme but I expect the gulls will have moved on when I next visit the town.

December 23rd I was up with the lark this morning to take the dogs for a walk through the wood at the back of the house. I love blustery winter days. The wind was whipping through the tops of the trees and as I walked, dead leaves were dancing around my feet like a flurry of snowflakes. I disturbed a flock of fieldfares and redwing from their roost in a tall hawthorn hedge and within seconds, they had been carried several hundred metres by the force of the wind. A passing female sparrowhawk had no chance as all the small birds were wisely keeping their heads down.

In the afternoon, I drove to Llyn Ebyr, a magical lake surrounded by woodland in the hills above Llanidloes. It's one of those places that goes completely unnoticed unless you're a local and know exactly how to get there.

WIGEON (photo: Steve Phillipps)

Today, the water was covered with wintering ducks large and small. As well as the usual mallard, moorhen and coot, there were over 50 teal, about 20 tufted duck, a handful of wigeon and one male pintail. The latter is a scarce visitor to the lakes of Montgomeryshire and when I do see one, it is invariably in the company of the much smaller teal. All these ducks kept to the safety of the vegetation on the far shore and I suspect that there has been some illegal shooting taking place around the lake as I came across several fresh shotgun cartridges. It's such a shame that the birds are not left alone because it's not a big lake and refuges like Llyn Ebyr are essential for these migratory ducks following their long flights from the far north.

December 25th Merry Christmas to you all! Just as I do every Christmas Day, I went for a run with the dogs in preparation for the huge dinner to come. It was a wonderful, cold morning and on the way to Gregynog, I passed two cock blackbirds knocking ten bells out of each other by the roadside. The season of goodwill obviously doesn't extend to blackbirds because both had lost a good few feathers before the vanquished retreated to the safety of a nearby holly tree.

Halfway along the run, the snow started to come down and towards the end of the eight kilometres, the dogs and I were running into a blizzard. Just as I reached the safety of the car, my eyes were drawn to a bramble bush where a male bullfinch was taking cover from the white-out, but try as he might, he couldn't get away from the biting wind. This was one of our local birds, not the larger and more pink northern bullfinches that have invaded the country in their thousands this year. One disadvantage of being one of our most brightly coloured birds is that you do stand out, especially in a snowstorm, and I wouldn't be surprised if he catches the attention of a passing sparrowhawk before the end of the day.

The afternoon was spent sledging in the back field with the boys but we stayed fairly close to the house because the far corner was snow-free, probably because it caught the rays of the midday sun, and full of hundreds of thrushes. Fieldfares and redwings were knee-deep, probing the mud for earthworms and other invertebrates, and occasionally flying up to an adjacent hedge to feed on the hawthorn berries. There must have been over 400 birds in total, all confined to an area about a quarter of the size of a football field. It was important for us not to disturb them because in sub-zero temperatures, a few mouthfuls of food can mean the difference between life and death to some of these birds.

December 26th The temperature dropped to minus six degrees Celsius last night and with a full moon and a sky full of stars, it was the perfect evening for a walk around the village. There wasn't a soul to be seen and it was so cold, even the tawny owls didn't dare raise their heads to hoot but at around 10 o'clock, just as I passed the church, a lone robin ventured forth to sing a few weak notes. Good on him.

Despite the snow and cold temperatures, there were signs of spring in the air, particularly the drumming of the great spotted woodpeckers in the wood at the back of the house. They had chosen a favourite perch where the hammering sound would carry for long distances to warn off any potential rivals for their territories. From now until early spring, the drumming will become more frequent until they drill a new hole and settle down to breed.

Later in the day, a woodpecker (possibly the same one) visited the garden to feed on the turkey fat I'd put out on a tree branch and having taken its fill, it drummed briefly on a telegraph post before flying off in the direction of the wood. On its arrival, all the small birds scattered to the shelter of the nearby bushes in order to avoid its dagger-like beak but as soon as it had gone, the blue tits were back on the fat once more.

December 27th This really will be remembered as the year of the Scandinavian invaders. As I drove towards the village of Tregynon this morning, fieldfares and redwing peeled off the hedgerow trees like dead leaves in the wind. Generally, these winter thrushes eat all our resident thrushes out of house and home before moving on to pastures new but this year, the abundance of fruits and berries has meant that they can remain with us throughout the winter without too much squabbling. Mind you, they must have eaten thousands of tons of berries because the hedgerows are nowhere near as laden as they were in the autumn and another cold spell may mean that the remainder will disappear as well. The conifers are full of goldcrests at the moment, tiny, busy birds that only weigh a few ounces. Like all small birds and mammals, they have to feed constantly and as their chief prey is insects and spiders, ivy-covered trees are always a good place to look for them. Although it is a fairly common breeding bird in Wales, thanks mainly to the spread of alien conifers, the winter population is greatly augmented by immigrants from the continent and it's incredible to think that our smallest bird can fly such long distances over water. Yet another of nature's many miracles.

Our resident pair of mistle thrushes have been conspicuous by their absence of late but this afternoon, they were back with a vengeance. They kept calling from the black poplar where they nested earlier this year and flying to the field at the back of the house to feed. From time to time, they visited the garden to feed on the remains of the Christmas pudding but it was the earthworms that really took their fancy.

December 28th The ice still hadn't completely disappeared from the canal this morning although there were plenty of open areas for the feeding wildfowl and herons. Hissing Sid's four surviving offspring are finally beginning to lose their brown immature feathers and replacing them with the resplendent white of the adults. At the moment, in the transition stage, they look like a two-tone tartan but by the spring, they'll be completely white, although the beaks will not yet have changed to the orange and black of the parents.

On the drive back from the canal, I killed a robin. It's been a very long time since I killed anything on the road and for a while, I felt quite saddened by the whole event, but as three-quarters of small birds die before reaching breeding age, you just have to accept it as being one of those unfortunate things that happens from time to time. In the past, I have killed some noteworthy species in my car, including the first recorded nightjar at the RSPB's Llyn Efyrnwy reserve. I had seen individuals feeding on moths along the river but the warden at the time refused to believe me. When I handed over a dead nightjar in a shoebox, however, he soon changed his tune.

December 29th It's funny how fate plays a hand in almost everything we do. Today, I'd intended taking the boys and dogs to the beach at Borth near Aberystwyth but once we reached Machynlleth, the weather was foul and didn't look as if it was going to improve. We therefore decided to eat in the café at Tre'r-ddôl but as the dogs needed a walk, I dropped the boys and their grandfather off and led the dogs up a short track which bisected a young mixed woodland.

In an area of brambles, young conifers and old birch trees, I could hear the weak calls of several bullfinches but as I approached, several dozen individuals flew up from the low vegetation, all with their bright white bums showing like beacons in the gloom. In all, there were at least 43 birds, the biggest flock of bullfinches I have ever seen in Wales. Just as I was about to leave, I looked up to see a large bird of prey with long wings and a long tail flying over the wood in the direction of Borth Bog.

It was a male hen harrier, one of our rarest and most beautiful birds of prey with its grey-blue coloured head, light grey body and black wing-tips.

I saw all of this in less than 15 minutes, and to think that I wouldn't even have stopped at the site had it been a sunny day!

December 30th I had intended to go for a run with the dogs this morning but it turned out to be a fairly lazy day and all I'd achieved by lunch-time, apart from a quick game of rugby with the boys, was to put eight more fat balls out for the birds. I don't have a bird table, mainly because I scatter all of our waste food along the base of the hedge and amongst the branches so that the small birds don't have to go far from cover to get at it. Once I put it out in the open, the crows and magpies devour it within seconds, if next door's dog doesn't get to it first.

Spring is definitely in the air. In Newtown this afternoon, I watched a male collared dove courting his mate by bowing his head repeatedly and cooing sweet nothings in her ear. At one point, he even offered her a twig but I think she knew it was still a little early to start nest-building and she proceeded to ignore him in that haughty manner that all females, no matter what species, appear to have perfected.

December 31st The final day of the year and a time for reflection as well as looking forward to the New Year. At present, the news is full of tales about the huge tidal wave that hit the countries bordering the Indian Ocean on Boxing Day and today's figures show that over 120,000 have been killed, although it has been suggested that the final death toll may exceed 200,000. At a time like this, it's difficult to turn one's mind to local matters but it does serve as a timely reminder of nature's immense powers and man's insignificance despite all his breast-beating and technological advances.

I had to go to Bala again this morning to get the MOT for the car so I took the dogs and Gareth Morgan, a local naturalist, with me. On the climb over the Berwyn moors, a flock of more than 60 stock doves flew over – a rare sight in this area. I read recently that this bird has been increasing over much of lowland Britain but in mid Wales, I believe numbers have dwindled over the past 25 years with the demise of seed crops. They may also have suffered from the removal of old, rotting trees because they nest in holes, like many of the owls, but I hope that a more enlightened grant system for farmers will encourage these doves to recolonize old haunts.

In some scrub on the edge of Llyn Tegid, I witnessed a remarkable power struggle. I was watching a treecreeper scurrying along a tree trunk like a vertical mouse when it landed on the floor and picked up an earthworm. Immediately, a blue tit appeared as if out of nowhere, picked up the other end of the earthworm in its beak and so began a brief tug of war with the poor worm as a living rope! It lasted no more than a few seconds until the blue tit gave up and the treecreeper flew onto the nearest tree where it proceeded to batter the earthworm by swinging it from side to side against the trunk.

As I write, dusk is falling and the ravens in the tall Scots pine across the field are very vocal. They are early nesters, timing their breeding cycle so that they have chicks in the nest when lambing is at its peak and there is plenty of food available. For some weeks now, they have been flying together as a pair, kronking loudly and indulging in some aerial acrobatics but soon, the real business of repairing the nest and egg laying will begin. Let's hope they and all of our wildlife enjoy a productive new year.

RAVEN (photo: Steve Phillipps)

TURKEY TO TALGARTH

'We came across a very unusual road-kill amongst the pine trees, a wild boar. These creatures thrive on the fruits, seeds and fungi in the mixed woodland and are rarely seen because of the thick scrub that carpets parts of the peninsula.'

Song Thrush (photo: Steve Phillipps)

January 1st It's time to be optimistic. The British government will finally give the countryside and its wildlife the respect and legal protection that it deserves. World leaders will pass measures to safeguard the future of pristine wilderness areas against mineral and oil exploration. And, who knows, even some of the better-known UK conservation organisations will put money, personal gain and politics to one side for the benefit of our plants and animals . . . Then I wake up.

The rooks were quarrelling in the tree-tops as I walked around Newtown park before daybreak this morning, no doubt squabbling over a few sticks as they start to repair their nests. Like ravens, they are early nesters, but they often roost near the rookery throughout the winter, especially if it's in a very sheltered area. Some of the older folk in Llanwddyn, the north Montgomeryshire village where I grew up, would tell me how rook pie was a staple part of their diet at certain times of the year. They would also eat a wide variety of birds' eggs, including those of black-headed gulls, lapwing and moorhen. We must remember that this was at a time when money was short, food was scarce and the birds were far more common than they are today.

Several people have told me that they have already seen daffodils and primroses in flower but here in mid Wales, I haven't even come across snowdrops in flower as yet. This morning, however, in a damp and shaded area of pasture, I found a large patch of flowering butterbur with its huge, rhubarb-like leaves. It gets its name because the thick leaves were once used to wrap butter in the days before refrigerators but in January, the leaves are nowhere to be seen because it is the flowers that emerge first. The flower spike looks like a small pink conifer and I was quite surprised by the numbers of insects that had been attracted to this plant on such a cool morning.

January 2nd It's been a few days since my last run, so, despite the protestations of my bones and muscles, off I went for a jog around the magnificent grounds of Gregynog Hall. There's a lovely mixed woodland around one of the ponds and in some tall alders I disturbed a flock of over 20 siskins. For much of the year, they are almost completely dependent on spruce trees for their food, tweaking the seeds from beneath the scales of the cones with their long, sturdy beaks. In the winter, however, they can often be seen feeding on alder and sometimes, birch.

Siskins are beautifully marked, or at least the males are stunning in their greens, yellows and black. Several people have told me that they get a great deal of pleasure from watching these acrobats feeding on peanuts or dandelion seeds in their gardens and coming across them on such a gloomy morning certainly cheered up my day.

January 4th Yet another visit to the Bala area, this time to interview Norman Closs-Parry, one of Wales's foremost anglers, on the importance of the river Dee for its wildlife. Mention the Dee to any birdwatcher and he'll tell you to visit the estuary where over 100,000 birds spend the winter months. Today, however, we were looking at the upper reaches of the river and even before we'd reached the water's edge, we came across a large flock of over 100 chaffinches and at least 20 brambling feeding under a line of tall beech. Despite an apparent influx elsewhere in

MALE CHAFFINCH

Britain, these were the first bramblings I'd seen this winter and it was a real treat to be able to watch the confiding males at close quarters. Similar to the closely related chaffinch, they have prominent white bums and pale bellies and the dark heads that characterise the males in their summer plumage can often be seen at the beginning and again towards the end of their stay with us.

We watched the birds for over a quarter of an hour before reluctantly moving on to the river itself. As soon as we arrived, three snipe exploded from the rushy ground beneath our feet and this set off a chain of scattering birds, including eight mallard and three red-breasted mergansers, a male and two females. The latter are scarce birds on Welsh rivers, unlike their cousins the goosander, and the Dee is one of the few inland waters where they breed annually.

As we walked along the banks, fieldfares and redwing galore were feeding on hawthorn berries on the opposite side of the river and upriver, we could see a flock of 18 goldeneye, attractive diving ducks that spend the winter with us here in Wales. The males are particularly striking with their green heads and large white wing bars and I'm hoping that it's only a matter of time before a pair stays here to breed. In northern Scotland, pairs were encouraged to breed by providing suitable nest boxes along rivers and lakes, and several organisations are now doing this in Wales. I've seen males displaying in early May on several Welsh rivers but, as yet, no breeding is known to have taken place.

January 5th This morning, I saw only my second woodcock of the winter. The dogs flushed it from a wide, bracken-covered ride in a conifer plantation and, on closer inspection, I could see where the bird had been probing into the soft mud in search of earthworms. It has an amazing beak because the end can open a few millimetres even when the bill is closed, the perfect tool for grasping worms that are deep underground. In the evening, I spoke to a colleague who shoots woodcock in west Wales every winter and he says that there are quite good numbers in some of the Pembrokeshire woodlands. Mind you, he does have two trained spaniels to do the hard work for him.

This time of year, winter is rapidly becoming spring. Along the Montgomeryshire Canal, the heart-shaped leaves of the lesser celandine have appeared almost overnight, pushing their way through last year's plant debris in search of sunlight. The towpath was covered

wild about the wild | turkey to talgarth

JANUARY

NUTHATCH

in them, whereas a week ago I couldn't find a single one. In parks and gardens, daffodils, snowdrops and crocuses are beginning to flower but it is the early wild flowers that I find most beautiful and now, I can't wait for spring to arrive.

There was a large movement of starlings this afternoon, probably because of the storm and gale-force winds that have been forecast for later in the day. Many of the news reports on the tsunami disaster in south-east Asia have commented on the fact that no large animals appear to have been killed and several eyewitnesses report seeing elephants moving to high ground immediately prior to the tidal wave hitting the beaches. I'm sure that animals have a sixth sense that warns them of forthcoming extreme events, or maybe their senses are just more attuned to such phenomena than ours. In days gone by, people would pay a great deal of attention to such things as the movements and actions of animals. It may be time to start watching closely once again.

January 6th I had to replenish the supply of fat balls along my hedge again this morning and within minutes, one of the resident nuthatches flew in to feed. They are the rugby props of the bird world – short, stocky, strong and very aggressive. With its dagger-like bill, it repelled all comers, including several birds larger than itself, and it also tore its way through about a quarter of the mixture of fat and seeds in less than half an hour. It's no wonder I have to buy so many at the moment.

January 7th They promised us storms and storms is what we got. The wind howled all day today, but at least the rain kept away long enough for me to visit the Dolydd Hafren nature reserve where the rivers Rhiw, Camlad and Severn all meet. It's owned and managed by the Montgomeryshire Wildlife Trust and is one of mid Wales's best-kept secrets.

The water level was high following two days' rain but thankfully, this meant that the reserve was full of wildfowl and devoid of people. The flocks of teal were, as always, skulking amongst the reeds in the oxbow lakes alongside the reed buntings and coots, but despite the perfect conditions, I didn't see a single water rail. These birds are secretive during the breeding season, keeping to the middle of the thickest reedbeds, but during the winter months they are far more visible and often venture out of the tall vegetation in search of food.

I'd taken my parents along to the reserve because they don't often get to see tree sparrow or snipe, two species that are usually quite easy to see at Dolydd Hafren. Thanks to the wind, however, the tree sparrows were keeping their heads down but we were able to watch three snipe probing the soft mud around the edges of the pools with their incredibly long beaks. They can be extremely difficult to spot as their brown and yellow plumage provides perfect camouflage for a bird that spends much of its time in or near mud and dull brown vegetation but, when disturbed, they explode from beneath your feet with a sudden 'giach' call that gives the bird one of its Welsh names.

January 8th The wind and rain continued unabated over much of Britain and areas such as Llanrwst in north Wales are flooded for the second time in under a year. We've been lucky here in Llandysul because although the wind has gusted for over 24 hours now, we've had relatively little rain. The pair of ravens that are setting up home in a large Scots pine in front of the house have made the most of the high winds, however, by displaying endlessly and playing above the fields. One of the pair tumbled whilst clutching a piece of wool, repeatedly catching the wool in its beak as it fell earthwards. They are one of the few birds that appear to fly because they can and because they enjoy it. If I came back to Earth as a bird, I could do far worse than returning as a raven.

On a walk around the lanes with the children in the afternoon, I watched a pair of stock doves prospecting for a nest site in an old oak tree. They are smaller than woodpigeons with more black and no white on the wings and, as hole nesters, they have to compete with tawny owls and kestrels amongst others. I used to see far more of these birds in the 1970s and 1980s than I do now and I suspect that, as with so many other seed-eating birds, it is connected to the demise of crops such as barley, oats and wheat. Still, with a pair prospecting on my doorstep, it's yet another thing to look forward to this spring.

January 9th More and more spring plants are beginning to emerge, amongst them cleavers, a scrambling plant which, as children, we would throw on each others' clothes and hair. Later in the spring, it will completely cover parts of our hedgerow bottoms. At the moment, however, the plants are only a few centimetres in height but even they add some welcome fresh greenery to an otherwise drab winter hedgerow full of greys and browns. It has several other names, including goosegrass, sticky willy and sweethearts, the latter because of its clinging habits. In Welsh, it's called *cacamwci* but we used to call it *caca mwnci*. I don't think I need to translate that for you!

Time now to pack my bags for a ten-day filming trip to the Dardanelles in Turkey. This will not be a wildlife shoot but a series on the First World War, although I'll be carrying my binoculars as I'm sure to come across something unusual.

January 11th I arrived in Istanbul, via Cardiff and Amsterdam, and was immediately struck by the capital city's magical mix of east and west. As we drove through the city towards the Gallipoli peninsula, mosques and minarets were jostling for position on the winter skyline with McDonalds and Burger King, modern-day skyscrapers dwarfing ancient castles and churches. The bird life amongst all this urban sprawl was reassuringly familiar – magpies, house sparrows, starlings and herring gulls. On this first day in Turkey, it didn't get any more exotic than the hooded crows that scavenged for edible morsels in parks, gardens and dark alleyways.

January 12th Last night, we drove south-west out of Istanbul, along the northern shores of the Sea of Marmara to the town of Eceabat.

MOUNTAIN STRAWBERRY

Unfortunately, I saw very little of the countryside as the majority of the journey was undertaken in the dark, but I did see enough to note that buzzards are extremely common in this part of Turkey with several birds perching along roadside posts, much as our birds do here in Wales.

The morning was spent around Anzac Cove on the Gallipoli peninsula, where the Australian and New Zealand troops came ashore in their thousands in 1915. It dawned on me as I walked around some of the immaculately kept war cemeteries that these poor soldiers were being better cared for in death than they were in life.

January 13th Higher up the hills overlooking the narrow channel known as the Dardanelles, we came across the bones of one of the thousands of soldiers killed in this battle 90 years ago. Bones are found every winter following heavy rain, so we dug a hole beneath a fruiting mountain strawberry bush, said a few words in English and Turkish and erected a rather rudimentary cross. As we gazed down on the last resting place of this unknown soldier, the sun came out and shone on the fruit-bearing bush as if some higher power also wanted to have its say in the ceremony.

We moved on to Sulva Bay, another battleground, where the British had been defeated by the Turks. Today, it's a wonderfully peaceful area of agricultural land full of olive groves and small arable fields but nearly a century ago it bore witness to yet another of man's senseless massacres. We filmed on an area called Chocolate Hill that overlooked the bay itself and a shallow salt lake which was full of large birds, probably geese of some sort, but I was too far away to be able to identify them.

An old man who lived in a nearby shack took us to see honey-bees which he kept not in modern hives but in hollowed-out logs wrapped in a kind of wicker basket. The honey was absolutely delicious although I had to share mine with the man's dogs, huge Anatolian sheepdogs that kept marauding wolves away from the flocks at night. Indeed, there were semi-wild dogs at every tourist attraction we visited, all of them friendly and well-cared-for.

January 15th Considering the slaughter that had taken place on the Gallipoli peninsula 90 years ago, the whole area is now remarkably peaceful and it's sobering to think that the Corsican pines and shrubs are flourishing, thanks, in part, to the bodies of those who died in the battle. This morning, we visited the village of Krithia where the Turks had mown down row after row of attacking soldiers using machine-guns. Today, the sound of guns and shells was replaced by crowing cockerels and squabbling house sparrows and the fields where so many of the British soldiers fell were full of feeding skylarks.

We came across a very unusual road-kill amongst the pine trees, a wild boar. These creatures thrive on the fruits, seeds and fungi in the mixed woodland and are rarely seen because of the thick scrub that carpets parts of the peninsula. At night, however, they wander out from the cover of the woodland to feed in the surrounding fields and it is here that they often come into conflict with man. The unfortunate individual by the roadside was a huge boar that had, by the look of him, come into contact with a speeding lorry.

As we returned to what could only loosely be called a hotel, I watched a female hen harrier quartering the arable fields in search of small birds or small mammals. Its slow, lazy wing beats belied its ability to turn suddenly on a penny and swoop down, its long legs at the ready, to grasp its prey. In Turkey, this bird is a winter visitor from its breeding grounds further north on the Russian steppes and Scandinavia. The dazzling white rump, which gives the bird its Welsh name of *boda tinwyn* ('white-bummed buzzard'), was clearly visible even in the gathering gloom.

WILD BOAR

January 16th Whilst filming at Seddulbahir Castle, overlooking the Dardanelles, I disturbed a male lesser kestrel that had been sheltering from the wind in one of the many holes created by shells fired from British warships. This is now a scarce bird over most of Europe although parts of Turkey still support good numbers. It is very similar to our own kestrel but the males have no spots on their chestnut-orange backs, their wings and tail are slightly shorter and they are smaller in size. On closer inspection, it was evident that the kestrel had been using the castle for quite some time and probably nested here. From its lookout, it was a short flight to the surrounding fields where it fed on large insects, small mammals and birds.

Small numbers of winter-plumage black-necked grebes had gathered in many of the shallow coastal bays, their bodies fluffed up like small balls against the biting northerly wind. In summer, they are attractive birds with their rusty flanks, black necks and back, golden ear tufts and bright red eyes but they are much more drab in their pied winter costume. Nonetheless, I rarely get the opportunity to see this bird at close quarters in Wales so when I wasn't needed by the film crew, I spent over an hour watching the grebes dive for their prey.

In the afternoon, we crossed the Dardanelles by ferry to the town of Carnakkale and en route, we watched a school of dolphins move gradually up the narrows, with three Turkish warships in the background. The dolphins would occasionally turn around and begin to fish as a group, herding their prey into a tight group before they all thrust forward into the middle of the shoal. There must have been at least ten individuals in the group, and we all watched them, completely mesmerised, until they swam out of view.

January 17th I was pleasantly surprised, during this visit, to discover that the majority of the Turkish people we met loved their animals. All the dogs appeared to be well-fed and the farm animals were well-cared-for. Last night, a racing pigeon had wandered into the hotel's bar area to seek shelter from the howling gale outside and rather than chase it back outside, the barman picked it up, fed it and allowed it to sleep near the fire for the night. The following morning, it appeared none the worse for its ordeal, and when the barman threw it into the air, it sped off eastwards.

This was our final morning on the peninsula before returning to Istanbul and much of it was spent around Anzac Cove once more. The beaches were full of dead crabs and shells that had been washed ashore by the gale and although most were quite familiar, there were one or two oddities also. I picked up a small white stone that had so many holes in it, it resembled a piece of cheese. At first, I thought the patterns had been made by the elements but, on closer inspection, I found a small shell in one of the holes. It was a teredo, a crustacean that burrows its way into rock, concrete and wood and I recall, some years ago, that the railway bridge across the Mawddach estuary in north-west Wales had to be rebuilt because this small creature had caused havoc in the stanchions of the old bridge.

January 18th We spent the day filming along the Bosporus in Istanbul amongst the black-headed gulls and cormorants. The city's skyline is magnificent, dominated by churches and mosques but even these tall buildings were dwarfed by the imposing Santa Sophia museum. Originally a church built by the Emperor Constantine in the fifth century, it was later converted to a mosque and, more recently, a museum. For over a thousand years, it was the largest enclosed space in the world. Today, it has lost some of its magnificence and inside, it looks rather the worse for wear.

Nonetheless, it is a striking edifice, particularly when it is lit up at night. One can imagine this huge building welcoming ancient traders, Greek conquerors, Crusaders and hundreds of generations of pilgrims. For

YOUNG CARRION CROW

me, the most striking sight of all was when a flock of herring gulls circled the large central dome in the eerie orange glow of the lights, like the pale ghosts of ancient spirits.

January 20th There was just enough time for a quick run around one of the Cardiff parks before spending the day in the studio. Although I've been out of the country for less than two weeks, it feels as if spring has accelerated into Wales in my absence. Robins, song thrushes and blackbirds were all singing before dawn and as the light improved, I could see a carpet of snowdrops beneath the bare lime trees. Winter is drawing to a close, but it may yet have a sting in the tail.

January 21st When I awoke this morning, there were hundreds of rooks and jackdaws feeding in the back field, like a scene from Alfred Hitchcock's famous film *The Birds*. The farmer has put more sheep in here recently, therefore the grass, which is usually kept quite long over the winter, is virtually non-existent. Contrary to popular belief, crows spend much of their time searching for invertebrates in the top few millimetres of soil, so short turf is very much to their advantage. The huge number of sheep we now have in Wales is the principal reason why so many of our corvids are so successful. Reduce the numbers of sheep and you'll reduce the crow population.

I walked around some of the rural lanes near Newtown and in the more sheltered areas I was surprised to find the lesser celandine in flower. The beautiful yellow flowers generally appear in February but every winter, in those areas where frost rarely reaches, some plants flower earlier than others. The Welsh name for this plant is *llygad Ebrill*, or 'April's eye', and this may indicate that flowers are now appearing earlier than they were a century ago, although I have seen little change over the past 30 years. Another plant that has pushed its way out of winter's grasp is the cuckoo pint or lords-and-ladies, as it is also known. In most areas, the leaves have yet to unfurl and still resemble green tubes but by Llanllwchaearn churchyard, beneath some tall beech, several leaves had opened fully.

January 22nd My first run around Gregynog Hall since returning from Turkey was not a pleasurable affair but at least I felt better having completed the five-mile course. I passed several flocks of chaffinches, totalling over 100 birds, with not a single brambling amongst them. It's a puzzle to me why they don't congregate in this area every year because the grounds of the great hall have some magnificent beech trees with a plentiful supply of seeds. Maybe next year.

Whereas the great tits had been thinking about spring around Newtown yesterday, Gregynog's great tits still had winter very much on their minds as they foraged amongst the hedgerows in the company of blue tits and a solitary treecreeper. Gregynog is in a shaded hollow and frosty mornings are the norm here at this time of year so flowers tend to appear that little bit later and birds generally nest a day or two later than their companions over the hill.

This afternoon, I saw my first new leaves, on a honeysuckle plant in the hedgerow near my home. The first, fresh leaves of a new year are always exciting finds, especially as they look so clean and perfect. Soon, the various caterpillars and other insects will begin to nibble away at them and by April they will have lost that newborn look.

January 24th It snowed yesterday, and today I was lucky enough to be filming in the uplands above the Tywi valley in Carmarthenshire, looking down at Llyn Brianne, or Llyn y Bryniau ('lake in the hills'), as it should be called. On a glorious winter's day, with the sun shining onto a freezing white landscape, I could see for miles towards Pembrokeshire, Cardiganshire and Powys.

These uplands are the spiritual home of the red kite. When this enigmatic bird of prey had disappeared from all other areas of Britain, a mere handful of pairs survived around Rhandir-mwyn in the upper Tywi valley. Some of those early nests have now been drowned beneath the waters of the lake but prior to the 1960s, this was a very remote area with only the drovers' roads for access. Indeed, it was this inaccessibility that helped save the red kite; that and the excellent work of local farmers and volunteer wardens. Today, of course, the red kite can be seen over most of Wales as well as large parts of England and Scotland but had it not been for the people of the upper Tywi valley, the kite's tale would have been a very different one.

January 25th A real red-letter day. Last night, a local nurse had telephoned me to say that she'd seen a waxwing outside Newtown hospital and could I please call by to confirm her sighting. As I had to drop the boys off at school, it was no trouble to call by the hospital on my way to record a wildlife programme for the radio, so at nine this morning, I was stood outside the main entrance with my binoculars at the ready.

I waited no more than two minutes before a flock of starling-like birds flew across from a tall lime tree to feed on the berries of a rowan in the hospital grounds. They may have looked like starlings in the air but once on the branches, there was no mistaking them for anything other than waxwings. Their pinky-orange plumage, dark mask and erect tuft were immediately obvious and, from close range, we could easily make out the yellow and red markings on the wing and tail.

Waxwings are stunning birds and the fact that this flock of 31 individuals was so confiding made it all the more memorable. The last time I had seen these birds in this country was near the village of Tregynon in 1989, so while other local birders came, saw and left, I stayed and enjoyed the view. The flock would feed voraciously before a territorial mistle thrush came down to chase them away. The birds would then retreat to the taller branches of the lime tree until the thrush moved on, then they would return to feed once more.

Whilst watching the waxwings, a male bullfinch joined in the feast, soon followed by a male and female blackcap. Thirty years ago, these dainty warblers were principally summer migrants from sub-Saharan Africa but these days, thousands of individuals stay in Britain throughout the winter, feeding principally on berries and seeds. They readily visit gardens and I generally see single birds skulking in amongst ivy plants, occasionally showing themselves when they come out to feed on the dark berries. It is only the male that has the characteristic black cap that has given this species its name; the female's cap is a rusty-brown colour.

January 26th In the evening, I travelled up to Plas Tan-y-Bwlch, the Snowdonia National Park's excellent study centre at Maentwrog in north-west Wales, to launch my new bird book. I wrote it over 12 months ago and it was a surreal experience to see the fruits of my labour appear in print. As a boy growing up in mid Wales, there was no Welsh bird book, therefore I hope that this guidebook will be used in every Welsh school in the country so that children today will know exactly which birds are visiting their gardens and that they'll be able to name them in both languages.

January 27th I travelled down to the village of Talgarth in Breconshire for a meeting with the BBC this morning but as I'd left early, I had enough time to walk the dogs en route. I stopped on the eastern side of the river Wye near Erwood on an area of common land covered by bracken and gorse. This area is full of whinchat, linnets and yellowhammers in the spring and even in winter, they support good numbers of stonechat and a few linnets. Such habitats are becoming increasingly rare, which is a real shame, because they are so rich in wildlife and they make ideal stopping-off areas to break up a long and monotonous journey.

On the return leg, I took the hill road over the Dolfor hills and I was horrified to find a dead hare on the verge. It was undoubtedly one of the animals I'd seen in exactly the same place a few weeks earlier but the circumstances couldn't have been more different. Then, I'd watched an animal in its prime. A creature that exuded power and speed with its long hind legs, sleek brown coat and large, alert ears. Today, I passed a heap of grey-brown fur and bones that had been unceremoniously dumped at the roadside having been killed by a passing car.

Only a few hundred metres along the same road, I passed the beech wood where I'd seen a handful of brambling outnumbered by 20 to one by chaffinches a month or so ago. This time, the ratio had been reversed. There were at least 150 brambling, probably twice that many, and watching the entire flock take flight was like witnessing a sudden

WHINCHAT (photo: Steve Phillipps)

blizzard as their striking white rumps retreated towards the lower branches of the trees. Where they had come from, and why they had chosen this particular site, I have no idea, but it was wonderful to see so many together, especially having just come across the dead hare a few seconds earlier.

January 28th The whooper swan flock at Aberhafesb on the outskirts of Newtown has now more than doubled in size. This morning, I counted 33 birds, including 13 youngsters, and a flock of over 400 Canada geese. Every year, the numbers of birds suddenly increases after Christmas but no one knows where the additional birds come from. I spoke with Kelvin Jones, the chap who monitors the large flock on the Glaslyn meadows near Porthmadog, and he says that they have more than 75 birds up there, the highest total he's ever recorded.

While walking up a small stream that runs through our village, I couldn't help but notice a small green plant that clung on to virtually every large crack in the stone wall that runs alongside the water course. This is the common wall rue, a member of the spleenwort family that loves old walls, bridges and brickwork of any kind, its curly tufts of leaves remaining green throughout the winter. It gets a great deal of nutrients from the mortar in the wall and when it grows in dense patches, I have found robin nests tucked away behind them.

January 29th I'm pleased to report that the first leaves are just beginning to appear on some of the hawthorn hedges around Newtown. On my way in to do my weekly radio programme this morning, the hedges on the outskirts of town had flecks of green in amongst the drab browns and greys and I'm sure the song thrushes knew that things were changing for the better because they were singing like a choir of Pavarottis.

Outside the radio studios, the rookery was full of bickering birds. I love rooks because they are amongst the most comical and quarrelsome birds in Britain. I watched them for at least half an hour and saw that as they repaired their nests, they appeared to have two different techniques for obtaining the sticks. The good neighbour would fly to a nearby tree or to the ground below to fetch new branches to repair last year's nest. In the meantime, the bad neighbour would wait for the good neighbour to disappear before jumping across to his nest to steal some of his sticks. Inevitably, he would be caught in the act of thieving and this would spark off another round of bickering.

On the way home, I watched a magpie carry a fairly substantial branch to the top of a Douglas fir. Magpies are amongst the best nest builders we have for they not only build a roof over the open cup, but also reinforce the stick nest with thick mud. I've heard many a farmer say that it's impossible to shoot a magpie off its nest because the mud dries like concrete and the wily bird either slips away while the farmer approaches with his gun or merely sits tight. They are not only beautiful birds but extremely intelligent as well.

January 30th Just enough time for a walk this morning before departing for Heathrow, then on to Sri Lanka via Qatar in the Middle East. Following the tsunami in late December, we had offered to postpone the trip but we were asked to carry on with our plans because the country desperately needs foreign tourists at the moment. There's no doubt that we'll also come across evidence of the effects of the huge tidal wave, so as well as my usual binoculars and camera, I'm taking a few colouring books and toys for the local schoolchildren.

When I return to Wales, I expect that spring will have taken a huge leap forward with early flowers and leaves along the hedgerows and the dawn chorus building up to its spring climax. Mind you, knowing my luck, I'll probably come back to three feet of snow!

COLOMBO TO CAERNARFON

'Primates aside, this was the day of the snakes. First was a huge five-metre python that had recently enjoyed a gigantic meal, judging by its size and reluctance to move out of the way of the traffic.'

ASIATIC ELEPHANT

February 1st I arrived late last night in Colombo, the Sri Lankan capital, and stayed in the luxury Galle Face Hotel. It was built in 1868 and remains a throwback to colonial times, but I had precious little time to enjoy the comforts on offer as we sped off across country in the early morning in order to avoid the city traffic.

We stopped to film at some wetlands on the outskirts of a town called Tissa in the south-east of the island where thousands of huge fruit bats, or flying foxes, were roosting in some of the larger trees and with their large eyes and furry bodies, it's not difficult to see how they've acquired their local name of 'dog face'. Whilst filming the bats, we almost stood on a two-metre rat snake, a harmless but agile reptile that immediately began to climb the nearest tree in search of prey – and make good its escape from prying camera crews, no doubt.

The wetland itself was full of birds, from white-throated kingfishers to the wonderful pheasant-tailed jacanas and whistling tree ducks, all attracted by the variety of plants, fish and invertebrates in the shallow waters. Several locals stopped to stare at the film crew, probably astounded by the fact that we'd flown thousands of miles to film a few birds on their local pond!

February 2nd Our welcoming committee to the Yala Village Hotel last night was an angry bull elephant, but thankfully our headlights scared it away before it could inflict any damage. We awoke early for our first look around the National Park which, at the tail-end of the wet season, was a rash of shallow lagoons full of basking crocodiles and wallowing buffalo, with waders such as yellow-wattled lapwing feeding along the shores.

Along the roadsides, four different species of bee-eaters would swoop alongside the Landrovers to catch large insects disturbed by our vehicles. The commonest species was the resident green bee-eater, but we also saw blue-tailed, chestnut-headed and European bee-eaters. The noisiest and most obvious of all the park's birds, however, was the peacock. Males would display in shaded areas along the tracks, the colourful, fanned-out tails a huge attraction to passing peahens and a visual threat to rival males. With large predators roaming around Yala in good numbers, it's surprising that such an ostentatious bird has survived for so long.

In the evening, we found a young male leopard relaxing in one of the uppermost branches of a tall tree, completely unperturbed by the presence of half a dozen vehicles full of gawping tourists. The large eyes, broad face and mottled coat make for a visually striking animal and it was a real privilege to be able to watch this eight-month old leopard at such close quarters. Nearby, according to our guide, the cub's mother and two sisters were hiding amongst the thick scrub but this young male certainly wasn't camera shy.

February 3rd At midday, when all the other birds and animals seemed to be enjoying their siesta, the langur monkey could be seen leaping from limb to limb, or just hanging around, on some of the lower bushes, feeding on leaves, seeds and fruits. In amongst one particular troop, it was easy to identify the dominant males and females, the moody teenagers and the mischievous youngsters. There's no doubt in my mind that Darwin was right. What is more, some of us are more closely related to the apes than others!

Primates aside, this was the day of the snakes. First was a huge five-metre python that had recently enjoyed a gigantic meal, judging by its size and reluctance to move out of the way of the traffic. Next came a beautiful Russel's viper with its diamond-patterned back. At first, I

RUSSEL'S VIPER

thought it was another young python and I was about to run my hand along its back when our guide pulled me back and explained that it was, in fact, one of the deadliest snakes in Sri Lanka. The haemorrhagic venom takes 45 minutes to kill a man; we were two hours from the nearest hospital.

February 4th This was a great day for leopards. I've seen lions and pumas in the wild but none match the leopard for sheer good looks and late morning, we came across a female and her cub skulking amongst the undergrowth, giving just tantalisingly short glimpses to Steve, the cameraman. Our guide, Ravi, is able to identify every leopard in the park from their unique facial spots but even he wasn't able to put a name to these two because of the all-too-brief views we had of them. Later in the day, we came across a large male leopard whom Ravi recognised as a five-year-old that had been born in the park and that, even as a cub, had been much bigger than his peers.

He stared back at us for several minutes before getting up and spraying his scent all over some nearby shrubs. We then saw a much smaller female emerge from the vegetation and take up a submissive pose with her belly flat against the short grass. The male mounted her briefly then walked away with her in tow, looking fleetingly over his shoulder at us as he went. I couldn't believe that we'd stumbled across a pair of mating leopards, nor could I believe the sheer size of this particular male. Ravi explained, however, that whereas buffalo, elephants and sloth bear will readily attack people if they feel threatened, attacks by leopards are very rare.

In the evening sunlight, we watched a herd of about 20 elephants feeding and playing in one of the lagoons. Two were very young, probably only a few months old, and they were careful not to stray too far from their protective mothers. There are fewer than 200 elephants in the whole of the 500-square-mile park and of these, only about 12 have decent sized tusks. These 'tuskers' have been heavily persecuted in the past for their ivory and, even today, poaching still occurs in the more remote areas of the park. Let's hope that the youngsters we watched will be left alone to grow to a ripe old age.

All in all, one of the best wildlife days I've ever had.

February 5th There's a mini-safari in my bathroom. On one wall, I've got a dark brown cricket, on another, a huge cockroach and a pseudo

wild about the wild | colombo to caernarfon

FEBRUARY

PAINTED STORK

scorpion has taken up residence beneath one of the loose tiles. This last creature is fascinating because it's like a large, flattened spider with two front legs adapted for grabbing prey. Up until this morning, they had all lived happily together but when I went in for a shower, I found the scorpion munching away at a cockroach almost twice its size. Indeed, it must have been an excellent meal because it's the last I saw of the scorpion!

There are some beautiful birds in Sri Lanka, from small sunbirds to the bee-eaters and the large storks, but my favourite, is the painted stork. It has a long, yellow beak, red head, white and black body and a beautiful pink patch near its tail. It feeds by walking through the shallows with its beak open and herding passing frogs or fish into it using its large feet. It's very common in Yala during the wet season, taking advantage of the plentiful supply of prey and good nesting sites in some of the tall trees growing in the water.

Wales play England at rugby today. I hope we win.

February 6th I woke up this morning to find 17 text messages on my phone and even before reading them, I knew Wales had won. To make things even better, BBC World News showed the Welsh try and the winning kick by Gavin Henson. I wore my Welsh flag with pride all day. How fitting, therefore, that this is a holiday weekend in Yala!

SLOTH BEAR

As the sun rose, I watched a pair of Indian rollers feeding their young in an old woodpecker hole. These are beautiful pink and turquoise birds, about the size of a jay, but it's only when they reveal bright blue wing flashes as they fly that you really appreciate how colourful they are. The energetic parents were back and forth every few minutes, thrusting food down the throats of the ever-hungry youngsters. With two growing boys at home, I know just how they feel.

In the evening, we had wonderful views of a nocturnal animal I really did not expect to see, a sloth bear. Despite its name, it is no slouch and although the individual we watched was completely unconcerned by our presence, the wardens at Yala will tell you that this is one of the most dangerous animals in the park. With its huge claws, generally used to dig out termites, it can cause a great deal of damage to the human body despite its relatively small size. About the size of a large Alsatian dog, they rarely venture out by day, so we were extremely lucky to come across the animal, especially one that was so confiding. What a wonderful way to complete our filming in the park, and a fitting ending to a wonderful week!

February 7th Our first lie-in of the week, getting up at 7am as opposed to the usual 4.30! It was also the first time we'd sampled the hotel's breakfast. But we didn't eat much. Sri Lanka's equivalent to Delhi Belly saw to that!

Having travelled to Yala across country, we returned to Colombo via the coast road which took us into the areas that had been worst hit by last December's tsunami. It was a sobering journey. Houses and shops had been completely flattened and ships weighing thousands of tonnes had been thrown like matchsticks hundreds of metres inland. It was very encouraging, however, to see that aid had reached even the remotest areas and that people were busy trying to reconstruct their homes and their lives as best they could. It was a reminder not only of the power of mother nature, but also the resilience of the human spirit.

We stopped briefly at a village near Galle, one of the worst hit areas, to eat lunch and I was amazed to see dozens of turtles swimming in the shallows, waiting for the sun to set before they ventured ashore to lay their eggs. In the animal world, as in the human world, life goes on.

February 9th No peace for the wicked. Following an exhausting 24-hour journey back from Colombo, I was out filming with Tony Cross of the Welsh Kite Trust this morning. Tony was erecting a video camera on a red kite's nest and the work had to be carried out before the pair started to repair last year's platform. The weather, wind and rain, was perfect for keeping the birds away as they generally start building on dry, fine mornings, and the work progressed without a hitch. Tony is great company, not only because of his vast knowledge and experience, but also because what you see with him is what you get. No hot air, no politics and no point-scoring, all of which are rife in most of Wales's conservation organisations today.

February 10th Spring is not as advanced as I had hoped it would be on my return from Asia. Admittedly a few primroses are beginning to rear

GOSHAWK (photo: Steve Phillipps)

their yellow heads on some hedge banks and daffodils are emerging quickly and will, hopefully, be at their best around St David's Day. Snowdrops are still looking good with blizzards of white flowers in some shaded woodlands. These, however, are not truly wild snowdrops but garden escapes, as are the daffodils that adorn the hedgerows of mid and north Wales. It is only in some parts of the south that you will see the truly wild species and even there, they are now very scarce.

I took the dogs for a walk through a mixed woodland near the hamlet of Garthmyl, between Newtown and Welshpool. From nowhere, a large female goshawk flew out of one of the Douglas firs and called briefly above my head before disappearing into the wood. This is a new site for these rare, but increasing birds of prey and it will be interesting to see whether this site will also be occupied later in the spring. In order to watch goshawks, it is best to sit at a site overlooking a mature conifer forest on a fine morning in March or early April because it is at this time of year that the birds are displaying prior to egg-laying. They are similar to the sparrowhawk only bigger with a more 'muscled' wing. Watch carefully and you may see the birds flash the white undertail feathers as they display – a wonderful sight.

February 12th All the honeysuckle in the woods around here are now in leaf although the hawthorns in our hedges haven't changed much over the past two weeks. When I went away to Sri Lanka, a few leaves were emerging but little appears to have changed. If we experience milder weather over the next week, I expect most of the hawthorns will leaf virtually overnight but who knows what the weather holds in store for us? Certainly the weather forecasters don't appear to have a clue as they predicted clear skies this weekend but pouring rain greeted me as I went for a morning run with the dogs.

February 14th What was that I said about weather forecasters? Yesterday, we had blizzards to add to the driving rain of the day before. It really was a miserable day because it was the kind of snow that melted quickly to leave a grey-brown sludge. The birds also hated it because they tucked their heads into their shoulders and squatted in the deepest recesses of the hedges for most of the day.

The snow didn't last long, however, and this morning, the whole family came with me to Bala where I was recording several pieces for the radio. On the way, we stopped to admire the beauty of the snow-capped peaks of the Berwyn moors. These are my favourite mountain range and although most of the wildlife retreats to the lower ground in winter, you can still find a few gems if you know where to look.

As the boys and I walked along a track that bisects some of the moorland, two male black grouse flew in front of us. They had been disturbed by a large male fox that wandered the moor with his nose to the ground, looking for any small mammal or bird unfortunate enough to cross his path. His coat was in immaculate condition and, even from a distance, I could see the wind ripple along his body. They have the most magnificent of tails which acts as a useful counterbalance when running at high speeds, or a snug blanket when lying up for the day.

A small pool surrounded by rushes and heather was obviously an important meeting point for the local frog population as it was full to the brim with spawn. It's incredible to think that these creatures can survive at over 300 metres above sea level on a bleak Welsh moor, not to mention mating and laying eggs in one of the coldest months of the year. As I disturbed some of the spawn, I saw several frogs hiding beneath the banks, males desperately clutching the females in a race to pass on their genes to the next generation. There was an unusually large number of dark brown and reddish individuals but I put this down to the peat-laden water rather than any pollution. Certainly, there was no shortage of frogs or healthy spawn.

February 15th If you ever get the opportunity to play golf on the Llanidloes golf course, take a few minutes to walk the beech woodland below you. I'm not a golfer myself, but I often walk the dogs through the woodland that abuts the course and no matter what time of year it is, I'm never disappointed. Today, chaffinches, robins, blackbirds and song thrushes were in fine voice and blue tits were busily casing each hole in every tree in preparation for the breeding season.

Someone had erected dozens of nesting boxes in the wood, all of them with small, round holes suitable for blue tits, pied flycatchers and redstarts. Most of them, however, had been attacked by a great spotted woodpecker as the holes had been greatly enlarged. We tend to think of woodpeckers as being peaceful creatures but the great spot, in particular, has a taste for chicks and he will go to great lengths to get at the nestlings. Some people put metal around the nest box entrance holes but the woodpeckers will then drill their way in from the sides. I now use nest boxes made of woodcrete, a solid substance rather like concrete, and to date, I have never had problems from woodpeckers or grey squirrels.

February 16th I had a good walk along the hedgerows around the village this morning and the changes since a week ago are startling. Not only are the common cleavers gaining height at an alarming rate in their annual quest for world domination, or at least verge domination, but other plants are also starting to appear. The dog's mercury that had poked their heads out of the soil a week ago are now several centimetres tall and pushing out spear-shaped leaves in all directions. These are shade-loving plants and they grow best in dark, deciduous woods where few other plants can survive the limited amount of light penetrating as far as the woodland floor.

Dog's mercury is a highly poisonous plant that, if eaten, can result in vomiting, kidney inflammation and, on rare occasions, death. It can spread rapidly using underground rhizomes and it grows so densely that it will shade out other, more light-demanding species. Although sometimes used as an indicator of ancient woodlands, I have often found it growing in woods that I know to be less than 100 years old. It is said that with the demise of coppicing and thinning, which would have opened up many woodlands in the past, dog's mercury is now on the increase in many areas.

Cow parsley is another plant that has suddenly shot up out of the ground in the past week or so, although the white compound flowers have yet to appear. Ground-ivy, on the other hand, is already flowering on many of the verges around here and although they are not the most obvious flowers in the world, the small, delicate, blue bugles are a wonderful addition to the late winter greys and browns.

February 17th I drive past a small heronry on the outskirts of Newtown at least once a week and I've been eagerly looking forward to the day when the birds would return to refurbish their large, stick nests. Thus far, I have been disappointed but this morning, five of the seven nests had birds on them and all were busily repairing the damage caused by the recent winds.

I'm always suprised to see huge, clumsy birds like herons in the uppermost branches of a tree and even more incredible is the fact that they nest so high up. On the continent, most herons and storks nest in reedbeds or in low bushes but our heron, the grey heron to give it its full title, always goes for the highest trees it can find. It's also a traditionalist, with generation after generation using the same nests, sometimes for several centuries.

Like rooks, they are early nesters and come March, the female will be sitting on four or five large blue eggs. In the past, I have seen whole heronries wiped out by summer storms but the most sickening incident I can remember dates back to the mid-1990s when three local lads shot over a dozen young herons out of their nests near Llanfair Caereinion in mid Wales, apparently because herons had been feeding on goldfish in a nearby pond. It's reassuring to know that we share this Earth with such compassionate individuals . . .

February 18th Today was a great day for buzzards. A cold, sunny day with strong winds at this time of year will always entice large numbers of this common bird of prey to circle and display above their future nesting woodlands. In one 15-kilometre stretch of road, I counted no fewer than 27 buzzards (someone else was driving!), several of which were displaying by folding their wings and swooping earthwards. They really are magnificent birds but here in Wales, we have become a little complacent about them because they are so common. I wish more people, especially birdwatchers, would stop once in a while to admire these wonderful acrobats and marvel at their ability to take advantage of the landscape and habitats created by modern agriculture.

BUZZARD (photo: Steve Phillipps)

February 19th I love my Saturday mornings because I have to get up before dawn to do a radio programme before taking the dogs for a walk. This invariably means that I'm out and about before first light and this morning was glorious with no wind, clear skies and bright sunlight. Every bird and every flower had that early spring aura about them and everything appeared to be celebrating the end of winter.

In nearby woodland, I could hardly believe that bluebell leaves had appeared and grown vigorously in the last few days although it will be another two months before the beautiful blue flowers appear. I recall being told by a botanist that in recent years, scientists have discovered a chemical in bluebells that could help in the fight against AIDS. I wonder how many more of our common plants hold the key to combating human ailments?

Talking of human ailments, last night I watched a documentary on global wildlife and George W. Bush. Why am I, once again, left thinking that all politicians are untrustworthy liars and cheats? Are they corrupt before they enter their chosen profession or is it the power that corrupts? Either way, they rank below slugs and slime mould on the evolutionary tree, only slightly above solicitors and local councillors!

I played rugby today, for the first time in several months, and helped Cobra Seconds through to the cup final in mid-April. My body is black and blue, but I feel that uplifting fatigue that only comes after a good, hard game of rugby.

February 20th Not far from our house is a wood that is slowly being transformed from a monoculture spruce woodland to a mixed native woodland and the incredible thing is that it's not owned by a conservation organisation but by a local resident. He told me that he would like to leave something for his grandchildren to enjoy long after he has taken his last breath and what better than a deciduous woodland? I walked through the wood this morning and it has a wonderful mix of oaks, ash and hazel with a rich ground flora of wood anemones, a few bluebells, brambles and plenty of honeysuckle. With so much honeysuckle, hazel and bramble, I wouldn't be surprised to find dormice colonising in the near future. We shall see.

Redwings and fieldfares are suddenly back with us again, no doubt preparing for their return journey to Scandinavia. When they first arrived in the autumn, they were very wary of people but now that they've spent a few months feeding on berries in farmland, parks and gardens, they are more confiding. It's wonderful to be able to approach close enough to see the bold, cream stripe above the redwing's eye and the grey head and rump of the fieldfare. In the autumn, they gorged on the plentiful supply of berries in our hedgerows before moving south and west for pastures new. Now that they've returned, they are spending most of their time feeding in mixed flocks on open fields, no doubt searching for earthworms and other soil invertebrates.

February 21st I haven't visited the Ynys-hir RSPB reserve on the Dyfi estuary for three years, so a radio programme on geese was a great excuse to return to this most beautiful corner of Wales. It is home to the only regular wintering flock of Greenland white-fronted geese in the whole of England and Wales, although large numbers can be found in parts of western Scotland and Ireland. These are fairly small grey geese with a white flash on the forehead, black bars on the belly and an orange beak. Or at least, that's what they look like when you get a good view; at Ynys-hir, they are invariably way out in the distance, grazing on the saltings or on the nearby agricultural land.

The geese used to overwinter on Cors Caron, Tregaron but in the severe winter of 1962-63, they suffered severe casualties and the few remnants moved to the Dyfi estuary. Gradually, numbers built up to a maximum of 179 in 1992 but, recently, the population has declined to under a hundred individuals with very few juveniles amongst them. Exactly what the problem is, nobody knows, but it is probably something to do with their breeding grounds in Greenland.

What was pleasing about Ynys-hir's geese, however, was the fact that the small flock of barnacle geese had increased to more than 130 individuals. These are lovely birds with their blue-grey bodies, bold black necks and bright white faces, and they are usually to be seen feeding in a tight flock, often in association with Canada or greylag geese. They first appeared on the Dyfi around 15 years ago and numbers have slowly increased each year and, in the long term, the hope is that agricultural land newly-acquired by the RSPB will benefit this and other wintering species.

February 22nd A phone-call from Dyfrig Jones of the Welsh Wildlife Trusts had taken me down to the Teifi marshes on the outskirts of Cardigan to see a young otter that had been abandoned by its mother. Dyfrig had hoped to keep it in an artificial holt where the mother might find it again but, by this morning, it was in an emaciated state and would have to be taken to a refuge centre near Llyn Syfaddan, Llan-gors.

The young otter was one of the cutest animals I have ever seen, with its chocolate brown fur, large whiskers and sleepy eyes. Indeed, if Dyfrig hadn't intervened, I'm sure the film crew would have taken it home with them! Unfortunately, abandoned young otters are frequently found wandering the river banks these days because of the alarming numbers of adult otters killed on our roads. Flash floods are also a problem as young otters are easily separated from their mothers and, unable to swim against the strong currents, they are often washed ashore miles downstream. Hopefully, this little otter will make a full recovery and, eventually, Dyfrig hopes that it will be returned to the wild somewhere near its natal area.

February 24th Yesterday was one of those exceptionally long working days that come along every now and again, where I leave home and travel to Cardiff before dawn and return after dark. Nonetheless, I did have time to note that the cherry and blackthorn blossom is out in some of the Cardiff parks and, as I crawled back up past Brecon in a snowstorm, a ghostly barn owl glided silently over the car.

When I awoke this morning, winter was back with a vengeance as a thick, white carpet of snow covered every hedgerow and field as far as the eye could see. The children loved it, of course, because it meant that they couldn't get to school, but the pioneer lesser celandines that had gambled on flowering early looked far less comfortable than the snowdrops whose white heads could still be seen peeking out from the hedge bottoms. My first task of the morning, after having taken a cup of tea to my wife as a special birthday treat, was to double the amount of fat balls in the garden. The effect was instantaneous as flocks of house sparrows and blue tits appeared as if from nowhere and even the battling robins briefly put aside their territorial differences.

February 25th For the first time since last weekend's bruising rugby match, I went for a long run around Gregynog. As you get older, knocks and bumps hurt more and last longer and my muscles complained bitterly every step of the way. At one point, as I passed a mixed oak and beech woodland, over a hundred woodpigeons exploded from the ground and such was the speed with which they took off, they left a ticker-tape of dry leaves in their wake. No doubt, they were searching for seeds hidden amongst the leaf litter, although, once disturbed, they flew directly down valley and into an arable field to continue feeding.

February 26th Last night, I drove up to stay with my mother and father in the village of Felinheli, between Caernarfon and Bangor, because I had to record a radio programme in Bangor this morning. I brought the boys along, but they woke me up at 5.30 this morning, so I went out early with the dogs. It was still dark and nothing stirred in the woods behind Bangor apart from a hooting pair of owls and a fox which had been noisily searching for scraps in some dustbins behind a kebab shop. By the time I left the radio studio, the night shift had gone home and the dawn chorus, accompanied by revving cars, had taken over.

In the afternoon, I left the children with their grandparents and took a walk along the river Seiont to Caernarfon Park where I was treated to the sight of two male mallards going at it hammer and tongs, battling over a female who watched dispassionately from deep water. One had its opponent's neck in a vice-like grip and was refusing to let go. In fact, so intent were they on their battle that I was able to walk right up to them until, after more than a minute, the victor momentarily opened his beak and allowed the vanquished to scuttle away to the other side of the pond. You really shouldn't get between a male mallard and his 'bird'.

On a quiet bay in the same pond, I watched a female goosander, most of its head underwater while it looked for fish. Or at least, I thought it was looking for fish. After a short dive, it actually came up with a frog in its beak and, having swallowed it, dived down again for another. In all, it caught three frogs before coming out onto a rock to preen. Although the books say that goosanders occasionally feed on frogs, this is the first time that I have witnessed it.

My mother showed me a robin carrying dried leaves to a hole in a wall where it was busily building its nest. Robins are great nest builders, not because of the nest itself but because of some of the places where they build it. In the past, I have seen robin nests in coat pockets, on car engines, in old teapots, in a half empty bag of sugar, and even one in the glove compartment of an old car. I often have great difficulty in finding their nests but my mum is a nest finder *par excellence*. When I was a lad growing up in Llanwddyn, she had found every blackbird, song thrush, dunnock and robin nest in our garden before I even knew they were carrying nesting material. In fact, I'm convinced that she knew where the birds were going to nest before the birds themselves did!

Another wonderful day for Welsh rugby with the team winning 24 – 18 out in Paris after a thrilling match. This could be our year for the Grand Slam after a barren run that has lasted 27 years. Let's hope so.

February 27th A part of the sewage farm on the outskirts of Newtown has been transformed into a nature reserve and although the smell isn't always pleasant if the wind is in the wrong direction, the birds love it. This morning, I stumbled across a flock of a dozen reed buntings feeding on a patch of waste ground that is usually overrun with weeds. In fact, the weed seeds are probably the reason why the birds were there because, on closer inspection, I could see small areas of disturbed ground where the buntings had been searching for food. I waited behind a thorn hedge nearby and watched as the birds came back and began feeding once more. In winter, the male's wonderful black head and moustache is covered by its winter feathers and it will not change into its breeding plumage for a few weeks yet.

February 28th I wish it would either snow enough to shut everything down or just give up the ghost as it's confusing me and the wildlife. Opposite the house, I've got a pair of ravens sitting on eggs with snow around the lip of the nest but a pair of dippers, that had been prospecting beneath an old stone road bridge, appear to have temporarily put all building plans on hold until the weather improves.

The pussy willows are out in force in a small area of wet woodland along a tributary of the Severn. These are actually the golden catkins of the male plants, called *gwyddau bach* (goslings) in Welsh, and the tree is a species of willow known as the sallow. Another common name for it is

ROBIN

goat willow, apparently because the earliest known engraving of this tree shows a goat eating the foliage. Willows in general are fascinating trees with dozens of different uses. Recently, they have been used by the Environment Agency on several Welsh rivers to protect banks that are being eroded by flood water and several living willow sculptures now adorn nature reserves throughout the country. Perhaps the most famous is the huge, four-metre-tall otter prominently situated outside the visitors' centre at the Teifi marshes reserve in south-west Wales.

This morning, I counted eight dabchicks together on one small pool situated in the crook of a Severn meander near the village of Llanllwchaearn. At this time of year, they are a dull mixture of grey and browns but they will soon be changing into their breeding plumage and dispersing to their breeding ponds throughout the Welsh lowlands. Here, they become extremely territorial and will attack any wandering dabchick that dares enter their territory. They also become very vocal, regularly uttering a long, bubbly cry from the depths of the reedbeds. For now, however, they remain quiet, tolerant and inconspicuous, concentrating on getting enough food to see them through what has turned out to be a long and wet winter.

ST DAVID AND THE APES

'Among the myriad birds and animals we're hoping to see out there are mountain gorillas, an animal I've wanted to see ever since I was a young boy watching Tarzan films on a Saturday morning.'

BABY GORILLA

March 1st *Dydd Gŵyl Dewi* or St David's Day and fittingly, the daffodils were fluttering in the breeze as I took the boys into school this morning. It also happens to be Dewi's seventh birthday today. He is a gentle soul and it's probably just as well that he wasn't christened Excalibur Saxon Slayer as I had originally intended!

March 2nd Despite the continuing flurries of snow, there are an increasing number of signs that spring is here – honest! On the way into Newtown today, I saw several pairs of collared doves displaying over their future nest sites. The males flap their wings to gain height quickly and then glide down onto a perch to woo the female. They can repeat the process dozens of times until she is perfectly happy with her choice of mate and nest location. Wood pigeons will also display in a similar way but they tend to fly that little bit higher and will fly up and glide down repeatedly. As a matter of fact, several birds undertake an aerial display above their nest sites in order to attract a mate and advertise their territory to rival males. At present, kites, goshawks and ravens are all displaying on fine, sunny mornings so it pays to get up just that little bit earlier to watch these aerial masters at work.

I leave this afternoon for ten days' filming in Uganda. Among the myriad birds and animals we're hoping to see out there are mountain gorillas, an animal I've wanted to see ever since I was a young boy watching Tarzan films on a Saturday morning.

March 4th Africa is a truly fascinating continent and the day-and-a-half's travelling is soon forgotten once we get to Uganda. The people are extraordinarily friendly and the children, in particular, are a joy to watch with their ready smiles. Travelling across the country, we passed several towns and villages where goat meat was cooked in roadside huts and salesmen sold everything from baby food to bananas, and from newspapers to pottery. By the end of the afternoon, we had reached Lake Mburo National Park, our first filming destination, and we immediately set off to make the most of the glorious evening light.

The park is like a small version of the Serengeti with a few more hills and trees and without the thousands of wildebeest or tourists. We had the whole place virtually to ourselves as we watched warthogs, buffalo and some particularly elegant zebras grazing by the dozen.

An hour before dusk, we came across a huge hippopotamus that had ventured out of the lake to feed on the short grass of a camp-site. They are massive creatures, the third largest land mammal after elephants and white rhinos, and to be able to drive so close to one was an experience I won't forget in a hurry. Hippos venture out of the water at night in order to escape the burning sun, and they will venture several kilometres from water in search of favoured grazing areas. This individual, however, was quite content to wander around the camp-site before returning to the water to rest.

March 5th Last night, we camped under the stars to the sound of hyaenas and hippos, but I must confess that I heard none of these sounds and my snoring probably kept many of the animals at bay. At first light, we were out filming along the edge of the lake where pied kingfishers vied for prime positions along overhanging branches. For over an hour, we watched an African fish eagle unsuccessfully attempt to catch the tilapia that ventured to the lake's surface to feed. Eventually, on the tenth attempt, it finally grasped one with its sharp talons and retreated to a nearby fig tree to feed. The pied kingfishers, it has to be said, were far better fishermen, catching fish at every third or fourth attempt on average.

In the afternoon, we moved on to the south-western corner of Uganda, to a much more mountainous area surrounded by farmland. En route, we filmed Uganda's national bird, the stunning grey-crowned crane. It is a huge, heron-size bird with sublime greys, whites, blacks and reds all

WARTHOG

over its body and a glorious golden crown to finish it off. On higher ground, white-naped ravens were common and every village had a healthy population of scavenging black kites, filling the role played by red kites all over Britain in centuries past.

We arrived at the Burundi Impenetrable Forest National Park after dark and descended a 300-metre slope along a slippery footpath in order to reach our camp site. Once we arrived, however, we were met by an Irish chap called Paul and several cold beers – the perfect welcome!

March 6th I woke up to the most breathtaking view of hillsides covered in tropical rain-forests. Even before I'd ventured out of my sleeping bag, I'd heard chimpanzees bickering and dozens of forest birds competing against each other in the dawn chorus. However, our sights were set on one animal: the mountain gorilla. There are no more than 700 individuals in the world and Burundi holds about half that population. But finding them can be hard work.

After breakfast, we set off with a group of trackers and porters along a narrow path that meandered up, down, then up again along a steep hillside. Eventually, we crossed a stream to find the 'beds' that had been made by the gorillas the previous evening. Every night, they bend a few branches together to form platforms where they sleep and once these have been located, the trackers follow their signs until they find the animals themselves.

Within the hour, we had found a group of about 21 individuals and after some careful work by our guides, we were able to watch, completely mesmerised, as a group of females and young fed on shoots and leaves. So engrossed were we by this spectacle that we almost forgot to film the animals and before we knew it, our time was up. Contact is kept to an absolute minimum: you are allowed one hour with the gorillas and can approach to within seven metres but no nearer.

With their grasping hands, intelligent expressions and loving caresses, the animals had been so human-like. Or maybe it is we who are so gorilla-like. But there is one pursuit where they beat us hands down: their diet of leaves and shoots makes for a great deal of wind and, believe me, an adult gorilla is probably the most ferocious farter in the world!

March 7th Yesterday's visit to the gorillas had been memorable but we had long since planned a second visit just in case we missed out on the

wild about the wild | st david and the apes

first attempt. This time, the troop had crossed the stream into a 'buffer zone' between the forest and farmland where the woodland wasn't quite as dense and therefore filming the animals was much easier. The dominant male, a huge animal with a silver back, was less shy than it had been the previous day and we were able to make out his immense size and incredible strength as he tore thick branches from trees as if they were matchsticks.

The youngsters were like human children: inquisitive and poorly behaved! They never wandered far from mother, however, and whenever one pushed his luck too far, a growl from the silverback soon

GORILLA

brought him back into line. It takes 30 years for a male to gain the silver colouring on its back and it can remain dominant for 15 years or more. Gorillas can live to be 50 years of age if left unmolested by man but poaching and habitat loss is a constant threat. In the past 15 years, however, numbers have shown a slight increase.

Once again, the hour passed all too quickly in the company of one of our closest living relatives. But my time with the mountain gorillas of Burundi was nothing less than a privilege and will remain vivid in the memory until I die.

March 8th The Queen Elizabeth National Park is situated in the Eastern Great Rift Valley, the cradle of man that extends from Lake Malawi in the south to Sudan in the north and lies in the shadow of the romantically named Mountains of the Moon.

As we drove through the park towards our hotel, we encountered a family of giant forest hogs, a kind of huge, hairy warthog. These are scarce animals and even lions think twice before tackling these beasts because of their fearsome nature and huge, upturned tusks. Dozens of fish eagles soared overhead and small herds of water buck, a large, grey antelope with long, straight horns, grazed the young leaves around the edges of the lower shrubs.

Violent thunderstorms in the late afternoon brought filming to a premature halt but it provided a spectacular show for all of us lucky enough to be in the park that evening. Despite having a clean, hotel bed for the first time in several nights, the heat meant that I slept fitfully and morning came much too soon.

March 9th An early morning drive took us to some of the remoter parts of the reserve and one area, in particular, which had been recently burned. Here, Uganda's national animal, the kob, could be found in large numbers feeding on the young grass shoots. It is a small, fawn-coloured antelope and the males defend territories in favoured areas so that the females can choose from dozens of suitable partners. This, however, makes the males vulnerable to predation and the presence of dozens of kob skulls scattered throughout the mating grounds was testament to the fact that lions and leopards had had many a successful hunt in this area.

In the fierce heat of the afternoon sun, we found a herd of over 30 elephants bathing and drinking along the banks of Lake George.

The African elephant is an awesome animal and two huge males in the herd were particularly impressive with their long tusks and imposing bulk. The group is led, however, by an old female elephant and it is she who decides when to leave the shelter of their feeding areas and move to the lake to drink. It is also the matriarch that decides when the herd leaves the lake to return to the scrublands, and a Welsh film crew was not going to block her exit! In the end, we reversed respectfully out of her way so that she could lead her group back into the bush. As I said, awesome!

In the evening, we found a large group of vultures squabbling over the remains of a lion kill and it was interesting to note how the larger lappet-faced vultures bullied the smaller white-backed and hooded vultures. It is from this kind of sorting out of the social structure that the term 'pecking order' comes.

March 10th I can't believe that we've reached our last day in Uganda so soon but, as with every trip, I am looking forward to seeing my family once again.

After an eventful journey on which we encountered hyaenas and the indiscriminatingly voracious marabou stork, we finally made it to the airport where we bade farewell to our excellent guide, Medi, who had been a wonderful companion throughout the trip. Ahead of us was a

AFRICAN ELEPHANTS

iolo williams | wild about the wild

long and weary journey of some 38 hours before we finally arrived back home in Wales.

March 12th It's surprising how little has changed in mid Wales over the past 10 days. The trees are still bare, the daffodils still in flower and the cold weather appears to have put spring on hold for most creatures. The snowdrops, however, are looking in a sorry state but neither lesser celandine nor wood anemones, two of the traditional early spring plants, are at their best yet.

MARABOU STORK

Frog-spawn has finally appeared in the pond at Gregynog, over a month later than the first spawn in west Wales, and some of the more sheltered larch trees are showing signs of coming into bud. In the garden, the birds are still coming in hordes to feed on the fat balls although blackbirds and song thrushes are far less conspicuous than they were when I left for Uganda. This probably means that they're sitting on eggs somewhere. When I find time, I'll have a good look around the surrounding hedgerows and lanes.

March 13th This morning, I heard my first bullfinch song of the year, although calling it a 'song' is rather flattering to this most beautiful of our woodland birds. It sounds like a wheezy, asthmatic barn door and no matter how often I hear it, I am always taken aback by the fact that such a beautiful bird can produce such a dreadful song. Indeed, its bright colours are probably impressive enough to attract a female and therefore it doesn't need to warble from the highest branches in the style of an avian Tom Jones. Whatever the reason for its excuse of a song, I can't help feeling that God is playing a joke on the poor bullfinch.

I can't pass today without commenting on the continued success of the Welsh rugby team in this year's Six Nations competition. This afternoon, they brushed aside Scotland in an enthralling first half in Murrayfield and next week, we meet Ireland in Cardiff for the Grand Slam.

March 15th I have just spent two foul days in the mountains around the village of Capel Curig in Snowdonia. We were trying to film along some of the web of footpaths that cross these mountains but gale-force winds and driving rain finally forced us into submission.

PALMATE NEWT (photo: Steve Phillipps)

I did have time, however, to explore a few small pools on the moor and discover that they not only held several balls of frog spawn, but also dozens of palmate newts. These small, lizard-like creatures love the acidic waters of the Welsh uplands and in a week or two, they will be laying their single eggs among some of the aquatic vegetation. The pools, however, had also attracted the attention of the local heron as one bank was scattered with the remains of frogs and newts.

March 16th I've always wanted to see our native Welsh daffodils and today, I met up with Ray Woods of the Countryside Council for Wales to search for two different species, the Tenby daffodil and the wild daffodil. We met at a remote churchyard in southern Ceredigion in the pouring rain, but the sight of hundreds of daffodils nestled amongst the gravestones soon made us forget the weather.

At one time, the Tenby daffodil was widespread over much of west Wales but in Victorian times, train-loads of bulbs were carried to markets in London. Gradually, they disappeared from most of their former haunts but recently, many of the local councils have put a great deal of effort into planting these native daffodils along the roadsides of Pembrokeshire and west Carmarthenshire.

The Tenby daffodil is a lovely little plant with its deep yellow flower and long, narrow leaves but equally striking is the wild daffodil with its larger, two-tone flower. These are also rare, and in Wales, are now confined mainly to deciduous woodlands in the south-east although small numbers still survive elsewhere. I, for one, will be planting nothing but wild daffodils in my garden in future in the hope that councils all over the country will follow suit.

It was interesting to note that daffodils were at their best in Llandudoch (St Dogmaels), as were the thousands of snowdrops that decorated many of the hedge banks. In mid Wales, the snowdrops are well past their best, whereas most of the daffodils have yet to show their beautiful yellow heads. This is because snowdrops need frosty weather to start their development, whereas daffodils rely on warmer soil temperatures. As the weather on the west coast is milder than it is inland and frosts are rare, snowdrops flower later and daffodils appear earlier than they do with us.

March 17th One of my first tasks when I joined the RSPB in March 1985 was to walk the major rivers of Wales to count the numbers of goosanders at that time. The results showed that there were around 70 pairs, the majority on the rivers Wye and Efyrnwy. Today, they are found on every major Welsh river and their tributaries, and this morning I counted three pairs along four kilometres of the Mochdre brook, a tributary of the Severn. I also found a pair of very vocal kingfishers chasing each other from branch to branch along a fairly deep section of the river. There is a suitable nesting bank nearby and I shall be keeping an eye out for this pair later in the spring.

March 18th This was the first true day of spring! With unbroken sunshine raising the temperature to a distinctly pleasant 18° Celsius, I was sweating profusely as I ran along the canal with the dogs and it was reassuring to see that Hissing Sid, the resident mute swan, and his partner, have nested near Aberbechan once more. A mute swan's nest is

like an enormous raft, constructed out of whatever water plants are available. When I ran past this morning, Mrs Sid was sitting proudly on her nest while Sid escorted the dogs and myself out of his territory, never taking his eyes off us for one second. He really is a great husband and no doubt he'll be back to his usual tricks of attacking innocent passers-by once the eggs hatch.

The sun has caused the mass emergence of primroses and lesser celandines all along our hedge banks. Lesser celandine flowers will open in bright sunlight and close once more at night or during periods of poor

PRIMROSE

light but today's fine weather has certainly accelerated the growth of leaves and flowers throughout the countryside. All of a sudden, hawthorn leaves are appearing on every hedge, larch buds have burst into life and the tangles of honeysuckle will soon be dense enough to provide shelter for nesting birds.

March 19th Having done my usual Saturday morning radio slot for Radio Cymru, I went for a walk through a mature, mixed woodland full of ramsons (wild garlic) and fresh bluebell leaves. The bone-dry leaves crunched under my feet as I walked through a stand of mature oaks and my ears pricked up at the sound of a goshawk calling from an adjacent block of Douglas fir. Immediately, however, the call turned into the repetitive strains of a male song thrush. They are excellent mimics, adding the calls of other birds to their repertoire in order to impress a listening female.

In the past, I have used the songs of skylarks to find pairs of golden plover and dunlin on the Welsh moors as these birds will also incorporate the calls of birds nesting nearby into their repertoires. But be warned, for I have been caught out many times by that most able of mimics, the starling. On numerous occasions, I have approached bushes and copses in the hope of finding unusual birds only to discover a male starling warbling away to his heart's content.

This was a historical day for all of us in Wales as our rugby team beat Ireland in Cardiff to win the Grand Slam for the first time in 27 years. I've completely lost my voice but I'm deliriously happy and very proud to be Welsh.

March 20th Another beautiful spring day and the old black poplar over the road is becoming the focus of attention for several birds. Just after dawn, a starling sang from the higher branches, a great spotted woodpecker was drumming on a dead branch, two nuthatches were alarm-calling around a potential nesting site and a pair of great tits have earmarked a hole for the forthcoming breeding season. How it will all end, I don't know, but there will undoubtedly be winners and losers. I'll keep you informed as the season progresses.

The first chiffchaff was singing in the hedgerow behind the house, having flown the 4,000 miles and more from south of the Sahara. It was a glorious day for advertising your arrival and he sang merrily for over two hours before taking a well-earned rest to recharge his batteries. It's incredible what warm weather and southerly winds can achieve at this time of year and I've no doubt that over the next few days, we'll be seeing sand martins and wheatear arriving on our shores in their thousands.

I walked the dogs around the Montgomeryshire Wildlife Trust's Pwll Penarth reserve on the outskirts of Newtown and witnessed something quite remarkable. At first, I thought I was watching a water vole feeding in the shallows of one of the ponds but closer inspection showed it to be the much smaller bank vole. Through my binoculars, I could see it struggling to feed on something just beneath the surface of the water before making its way back to land. Once ashore, another bank vole swam out to exactly the same spot and repeated the process.

I watched for a few minutes until both voles had disappeared into the long grass at the edge of the pond and then I walked as close as possible to the site where they had been feeding. Just beneath the water, less than a metre from the bank, were bundles of frog-spawn with newly emerged tadpoles basking in the sun. The voles had been feeding either on the spawn or the tadpoles, or both, and making repeated visits to reach their food. The books I have in my library tell me that bank voles are almost wholly herbivorous but they will occasionally feed on insects and earthworms. There is no mention anywhere of frog-spawn or tadpoles.

This is one of the wonderful things about watching wildlife; you never know when you'll come across something new.

March 21st I arrived back home from Teifi marshes (where I'd been attracting water rail out of the reeds by playing a tape of a calling male!) to find dozens of toads crossing the lane outside our house in order to reach next door's pond. The light drizzle and warmer temperatures had lured them out of their hibernation sites but, unfortunately, several had already been killed by passing cars. I hurriedly put together a salvage crew made up of myself and my two young sons and within minutes, we were picking up toads by the handful and releasing them in the pond. The still night air was full of croaking toads and my youngest son, Tomos, proved very adept at carrying them four at a time to their breeding pool. We all went to bed that night feeling that, for once, we'd actually done something positive to help the area's wildlife.

March 22nd On the way back from a radio recording near Llanidloes, I stopped off at a huge area of shingle and gorse at Llandinam. Here, I saw my first little-ringed plover of the year, a small wading bird which resembles the coastal ringed plover, but without the obvious white stripes in the wing and bright orange beak. It is one of the first migrants to arrive back from Africa and, in Wales, it nests mainly on shingle banks along our major rivers. It is quite common along the Severn and the Tywi in south-west Wales, but fairly scarce elsewhere.

The boys and I went out on toad patrol again this evening but there were fewer of them on the road, possibly because it's a clear, dry night. Some of the toads had already paired up long before reaching next door's pond, the smaller males clinging on to the females for dear life with their front feet, leaving the stronger back legs free to kick off any potential rivals. It's a very homely and comforting experience at the moment to go out for a walk at night and hear a choir of toads croaking contentedly for hours on end.

March 23rd I spent the afternoon and evening filming the raven roost at Newborough Forest on Anglesey with Nigel Brown, one of the best all-round naturalists in the whole of Wales. Nigel has forgotten more than I will ever know about the natural world and there isn't a plant, bird or insect on Anglesey that he can't identify. He's also been one of the key people involved in the counts of ravens and other crows at the Newborough roost, the second largest in the world.

TOAD (photo: Steve Phillipps)

Nigel explained that the birds probably congregate from as far afield as Ireland, the Lake District and the south-west of England and that the roost is an important social gathering for these birds. At dusk, we watched dozens of ravens congregate around a small pool in a clearing in the forest where they had a good wash before finally retreating into the uppermost branches of some Corsican pines for the night. It was fascinating to listen to the various grunts, wheezes and kronks that ravens make as they communicate with each other and I'm sure that had we been able to understand raven language, some birds would be telling relatives and friends where to find the best feeding sites, whereas others would be whispering sweet nothings in their potential partner's ear.

I stayed the night in a motel near Chester and as we arrived, I watched a barn owl hunting over a weedy field near the busy A55 dual carriageway. I hoped I wouldn't find the same bird in a heap of feathers along the roadside the following morning.

March 24th The barn owl must have made it home safely because there was no sign of him as I set off towards Deeside at 6 o'clock this morning. I was heading for Beeches Farm, a 400-acre mixed farm that sits on the flood-plain along the Dee. It is managed by Stephen and Anne Wrench and their son John, and largely because of their way of farming, it is a haven for wildlife.

As I arrived, I watched dozens of lapwings displaying over the ploughed fields, whilst hares were chasing each other along the furrows before boxing for a few seconds, then taking up the chase once more. Tree sparrows were squabbling amongst the hawthorn branches and male yellowhammers, resplendent in their bright yellow plumage, were singing to their hearts' content from the topmost branches of the hedgerow oaks. Flocks of linnets flew from one weedy corner to the next, a pair of curlew was setting up territory in an adjacent field and the air was full of the song of skylarks.

This is no exaggeration. The land is an oasis for wildlife that has declined severely over much of Britain and yet thrives at Beeches Farm because traditional methods of mixed farming have been maintained. The Wrench family use modern agricultural methods and make a decent living without having had large grants from the various conservation organisations. Later in the spring, I shall be returning to film other scarce birds such as grey partridge, swallows and house sparrows, all of which are common on the farm. It really is an inspirational place.

March 26th The hedgerows are now alive with flowers with the primroses, daffodils and wood anemones joined by lesser stitchwort and, in the grassier verges, dandelions. Tomos, our youngest son, keeps bringing daisies into the house for his mother and despite several explanations on the perils of picking flowers, the gifts continue to arrive daily.

Nests are late here in mid Wales, probably because the late snow and cold weather delayed the appearance of leaves, but my mother reports that in Felinheli, near Bangor, robins, blackbirds and song thrushes have been sitting on eggs for several weeks. Three years ago, when the leaves appeared very late, several song thrush and blackbird nests were predated by magpies because they were so easy to find in the bare hedgerows. This year, many of the leaf buds have been stripped by idiotic landowners and councils who have already been flailing hedgerows.

In the afternoon, we had our first significant rain for several weeks and the resident house sparrows duly celebrated by bathing noisily in next door's pond. The toads were also happy with the damp weather and since the boys and I started our toad patrol several nights ago, over 40 have been picked up from the lane and the numbers killed have been greatly reduced. Let's hope that this translates into more toads hatching later in the year, especially as I have plans to create a pond in our garden over the summer and it would be wonderful to be able to watch them breed here next spring.

March 27th Well done, Powys County Council! They have finally agreed to close a minor road that circumnavigates the lake at Llandrindod Wells after years of campaigning by the local wildlife trust. The problem is that thousands of toads hibernate in an adjacent woodland and every spring, they cross the minor road in order to reach the lake. Hundreds are killed and despite constant pressure from conservationists, they have refused to close the road until now. In the meantime, partly because of the huge number of road deaths, the number of toads has declined from 10,000 to 3,000.

March 28th Anyone visiting our house would think that we have several pairs of curlew breeding in the surrounding fields but, unfortunately, this is not true. We have a male starling that mimics a calling curlew perfectly and two of the resident male song thrushes have now copied him and included the curlew's song in their repertoire.

The end result is a choir of calling curlews, none of which are actually curlews.

March 29th My brother and his family have come up from St Albans to stay with us for a few days and as he grew up in mid Wales, he misses the countryside and its wildlife. He and I took his two and my two boys down to the river Severn and along a long, narrow island which is great for wildlife and a natural adventure park for kids. Although they spent much of their time throwing stones into the water, they were fascinated by the fish and invertebrates we found hiding beneath stones on the river bed.

Bullheads were very common, as were stonefly and caddis fly larvae but their favourite was the frog-spawn that we found in a small pond surrounded by beautiful marsh marigolds. By now, the tadpoles have emerged and are busily eating their way through the jelly and all the boys enjoyed holding some of the spawn in their hands before putting it back in the water. We also found a newly built long-tailed tit nest with its moss and lichen camouflage, and a blackbird had laid one egg in her cup nest hidden among flotsam left high and dry by the winter floods. It was wonderful to watch their eyes light up as they explored every nook and cranny on the island and it must have been comforting for my brother to see his sons enjoying themselves without the constant worry of speeding cars or suspicious men.

In the evening, a local naturalist called Gareth Morgan took all of us to see a badger sett that he's been visiting for over 20 years and where the animals have become so accustomed to him that they readily take food from his hands. We were not disappointed because in all, we saw 12 badgers wandering around the sett in search of the peanuts that Gareth had scattered over the floor. The only dampener on an otherwise excellent evening was the discovery of a dead badger adjacent to one of the entrance holes. It was Scratcher, an individual that Gareth had known for over 12 years and although it was sad to find him dead, at least he'd lived a long and full life.

March 31st Yesterday was the wettest and most miserable day of the year!

This morning proved to be dull and rather foggy but at least the rain had stopped, giving the bees time to scurry around in search of nectar. Many of the roadside flowers looked very bedraggled, the lesser celandines having closed down for the duration and the wood anemones hanging their heads in shame. The native plants had fared better than many of the exotics, however, as hundreds of daffodils planted on the verges around the village had been flattened by the 24-hour cloudburst.

BADGER

TURTLES AND DRAGONS

'A few hundred metres further on, we were startled by a flash of black closely followed by a streak of blue – a male sparrowhawk pursuing a male blackbird.'

LESSER CELANDINE

April 1st What a difference a day makes! March may have gone out like a damp squib but April came in with a ray of sunshine. The lesser celandines that looked so sorry for themselves yesterday are reaching out for the sunshine and opening their flowers to the full. With daffodils, dandelions and coltsfoot galore, the hedge banks along the river Severn were a sea of yellow.

In amongst a hawthorn thicket, I heard my first willow warbler of the year although it did not reveal itself despite all my best efforts. A friend I met by the river had seen three swallows earlier that morning but I saw no sign of them nor of the lesser-spotted woodpecker that had apparently been calling from a row of alders along the water's edge. I did, however, see and hear a very vocal male green woodpecker that was advertising its territory for all and sundry from the branches of a tall willow. It has plenty of invertebrate food in an ancient meadow nearby, so I hope he succeeds in attracting a mate.

April 2nd The best day of the year so far with early mist belying the unbroken sunshine that would be enjoyed throughout the country. On the way back from doing my weekly radio slot, I passed by Aberhafesb to count the whooper swans in the fields adjacent to the river. Earlier in the year, I had counted a maximum of 33 but by now, many have already started the long journey north to Iceland and I counted only 12 this morning. Another week or so and all the swans will have moved on before returning once more in the autumn.

Thick mist can sometimes be very useful for watching wildlife, especially if you sit in one place and wait. This evening, the mist had returned and I sat with the dogs underneath Aber-miwl bridge to listen to the evening chorus of rooks, song thrushes and robins. Suddenly, a fox crept out of some thick brambles a few metres to my left and walked up the bank in search of any food washed up by the midweek flood water. It was completely oblivious to the dogs and myself, as was a roosting cormorant which almost had a heart attack when it was disturbed by the fox. The mist had hidden us completely, allowing me to get nearer than I have ever been before to a very shy and very beautiful animal.

April 3rd We enjoyed some of Wales's best scenery today. In the company of our friends Steve and Anne of Abergavenny, we took a short walk along the river Usk where spring seems so much more advanced than it is at home. The wildlife was excellent too and Steve was able to show our kids a grey wagtail's nest in a rotten tree branch and a female goosander returning to her nest high up in a hollow beech. The kids are convinced that he is the original Crocodile Dundee and having spent a day in the field with him, I'm inclined to agree. They were particularly impressed by Steve's ability to catch shrews, voles and, slow-worms under sheets of corrugated iron that he'd put out on a warm, south-facing bank. No doubt, Dad will now have to do something similar for them in mid Wales.

On the way back to Steve's house, we met a man from Pont-y-pŵl who had been searching for ancient coins and other artefacts in the local area. In just a few hours, he had found several coins dating from as far back as the Middle Ages and a beautiful silver coin from the reign of William III in the seventeenth century. Just as with naturalists, it's surprising what you can find under your feet if you know what you're looking for.

April 5th A quick walk along some of the lanes around the house before heading off to Indonesia via Heathrow and Singapore. I'm more convinced than ever that many birds delay egg-laying when leaves emerge late because, this morning, I found two blackbird nests and a robin's nest in the most ridiculous of places. All three had been placed amongst sparse ivy on a rocky verge and all were very easy to find. There were, as yet, no eggs in two of them but the remaining blackbird nest contained two cold eggs, indicating that she has not finished laying.

Further along, a pair of blackbirds had decided to go ahead and lay in an exposed nest placed in a hazel hedgerow. The inevitable had happened, however, as the cup contained two predated eggs and other bits of eggshell. Closer inspection revealed peck marks on the eggs, a sure sign that a member of the crow family, probably a magpie, had been responsible. I now go abroad for ten days but I shall inspect the remaining nests when I return to record their progress.

April 8th It's taken three whole days to get to a boat on the Java Sea, but it's been well worth it! We flew overnight to Singapore, then on to a hotel in Bali, before flying again to the west of the island of Flores to catch the boat that will take us around some of the smaller Indonesian islands. Expecting little more than a bath-tub, we were overjoyed to find that because the boat we'd booked had broken down, we had been upgraded at no extra expense, and what an upgrade! We have en suite cabins and all our meals cooked for us – sheer luxury!

We were up early this morning to land on the island of Rinca, one of only four islands in the world where the huge monitor lizards, known as

Komodo dragons, live. Up until 1992, tourists were encouraged to bring dead goats and chickens across to Komodo and Rinca in order to use it as bait to attract the giant lizards but today, thankfully, this has been banned.

One of the rangers led us on a walk around the largely treeless island and although we came across an irate water buffalo wallowing in a pool of mud and several white-breasted tree swallows feeding like flycatchers around the branches of a solitary tree, we didn't manage to get close views of any dragons. We needn't have worried, however, because as we returned to the warden's cabins, we came across a patch of bare earth where eight of these huge creatures were sunbathing, two of which were almost three metres in length.

They really are a throwback to the days of the dinosaurs and it's a miracle that they have survived for so long without being over-exploited by man. I felt like one of the scientists from the film *Jurassic Park*, visiting an island that time forgot. We had now acquired three wardens with cleft sticks to protect us and as one of the large male dragons was particularly aggressive, we were very glad to have them. Komodo dragons are surprisingly agile creatures with the ability to run at up to 20 kilometres per hour. They are therefore a formidable predator and woe betide any careless pig, deer or buffalo that wanders too close.

SHIP ANCHORED OFF KOMODO

Generally, they ambush their prey by lying in wait alongside paths and tracks and whereas smaller prey will be dispatched immediately, they have a different technique altogether for dealing with animals such as deer and buffalo. Their teeth are serrated in order to tear flesh and they possess an extremely toxic saliva full of dangerous bacteria. They drool constantly and one bite will lead to a festering wound that will, within 48 hours, lead to the death of any large animal. Man also features on the prey list, by the way, and the odd, unwary tourist has fallen victim in the past.

In the late afternoon, a swim in the beautiful, blue seas washed away the morning's grime and we later moved on to anchor off the island of Komodo.

April 9th Most of the small Indonesian islands we saw as we sailed west were largely devoid of trees as the ancient tropical rain-forests had been cleared by man over the past few centuries. Komodo is different in that it has retained some wooded areas and as such, it supports relatively large numbers of birds such as yellow-crested cockatoos and friarbirds as well as rusa deer. These are similar to red deer in colour and size, and form an important prey item for the dragons that live on the island.

KOMODO DRAGON

Several of the lizards we saw in the afternoon carried radio transmitters on their backs as part of a study into their movements by students from the University of Santiago in Chile. It says a great deal about the state of nature conservation in south-east Asia when studies have to be funded by a university that is about as far from Komodo as you can get.

In the evening, the rain subsided and I spent several hours snorkelling and filming around a coral reef. The diversity of life was incredible with several dozen species of coral supporting hundreds of different fish and other wildlife. Brain corals, fan corals and dozens of others I simply couldn't name, provided homes for sea anemones, sea cucumbers, large blue starfishes and the most colourful fish you can imagine. These ranged from the familiar clown-fish, made famous by the film *Finding Nemo*, as well as the equally exotic blue devils, pipe-fish and angel-fish. It was like swimming in an aquarium.

April 10th The coral reef proved so popular last night that the film crew and myself all went back again this morning. It was pouring with rain and fairly cool but underwater, it was warm and clear. As we swam back towards the boat, six magnificent frigate-birds circled overhead like huge red kites. They are pirates of the open sea, chasing fish-eating birds remorselessly until they regurgitate their 'cargo' of half-digested fish which the frigate-birds then pluck from the surface of the ocean. A perfect start to the day!

Later, we sailed back to Flores and travelled, via Bali, to west Java. Here, we set up base at Rose's Ecolodge near the boundary of the Baluran National Park, an area of tropical forest, savannah and mangrove swamps centred around an extinct volcano.

April 11th On the edge of the mangroves, we encountered a large troop of long-tailed macaques and I watched, fascinated, as several youngsters dived underwater in search of food. Occasionally, they would surface with seeds in their hands and they would then retreat

MACAQUE

to some of the uppermost branches to dry out and enjoy their hard-earned fare. One male was extremely aggressive, probably because he is so used to being fed by passing tourists, and he made several dummy runs towards me as I photographed him, sometimes baring his teeth as an added threat.

Returning to our guest-house, we ran the gauntlet of a busy Indonesian road and its most feared animal, the Asian bus driver. Anyone who wants to surpass the adrenaline rush of an Alton Towers white-knuckle ride should travel across Indonesia by bus. Odds-on they would never make it.

April 12th Out very early this morning to film the sun rising above the park. The sunrise itself was spectacular but the wildlife was notable by its absence.

At midday, we drove south across the island to reach Meru Betiri National Park, an area of lowland rain-forest and unspoilt beaches dominated by yet another volcano, Gurung Betiri. The final 15 kilometres involved driving along the roughest track imaginable so that by the time we arrived, every single joint in my body needed tightening. To our horror, we found that our guest-house had no running water, no electricity and hardly any food other than rice, rice and more rice.

Arriving after dark, I was welcomed by a praying mantis, several lizard-like geckos and a small rat that had set up home in one of my skirting-boards. This was the most wildlife I'd seen for several days.

April 13th A lie-in – until 8am! Then, after yet another breakfast of rice, we went for a walk along the edge of the forest and into the adjacent village of Sukamade. The tropical forest was impressive but the fauna was not. We saw no more than four different species of birds and the whole place was eerily quiet.

Our visit to the village partly explained this as every home we passed had at least two caged birds, with some having over half a dozen. All were extremely colourful, such as the stunning azure-blue Asian fairy bluebird, beautiful lime-green leaf-birds or the strikingly-coloured orange-headed thrush. Hornbills and mynahs were also popular as were shrikes and starlings. All these are now extremely scarce throughout the country. And if the lack of financial support for conservation and the corruption in local government that I had already witnessed in south-east Asia were anything to go by, what hope for many species of plants and animals in Indonesia?

My heart was lifted in the late evening, however, as we filmed a female green turtle coming ashore to lay her eggs. These are magnificent creatures that spend the majority of their long lives at sea, returning to land only briefly every two years in order to lay their 100 or so eggs. It's incredible to think that these reptiles have been around for millions of years, long before the large dinosaurs walked the earth, and that the same isolated beaches are used year after year for centuries.

95% of the young turtles will die in their first year and if they live long enough, they will reach sexual maturity when they are about 20 years old. The females then return to the very beaches where they were born to lay their soft-shelled eggs coated in a natural pesticide and if they are lucky, they may live to be 70 or more years old. It took a full four hours between when our female first emerged from the water and when she finally disappeared beneath the crashing waves. I felt humbled and privileged to be able to witness such a unique occasion and I sincerely hope her offspring will be allowed to return to this isolated beach for millennia to come.

April 14th My hopelessness about the future of nature conservation in Indonesia was encapsulated by my farewell image of the Meru Betiri National Park. Several decades ago, the authorities had built a

TURTLE

magnificent statue of its then flagship species, the now extinct Javan tiger. Today, the tiger stands headless, covered in graffiti and surrounded by rubbish.

April 16th Despite, or probably because of jet-lag, I was wide awake at 5am, having enjoyed just four hours sleep. There was nothing for it but to walk the dogs. Almost two weeks have passed since I was here last but everywhere looks virtually the same as when I left.

Even the dawn chorus had a familiar ring to it with blackbirds, song thrushes and robins to the fore although great tits and chaffinches were far more vocal than they had been at the beginning of the month. A quick inspection of my nest boxes showed that two were already occupied although the pairs of great and blue tits had not yet laid any eggs.

In the afternoon, I played in the mid-Wales league cup final and I knew we were going to win when, at half time, a kite circled low above the centre of the field before drifting away towards a nearby woodland. The victory was all the sweeter for having lost in last year's final, but I was too shattered to join in the boozy celebrations. I really am getting too old for this game.

April 17th I drove up to north Wales to help celebrate Conwy RSPB reserve's 10th anniversary. Originally constructed from spoil dumped after the construction of the Conwy A55 tunnel, today the reserve is a magnificent oasis for wildlife with its backdrop of the estuary, the Carneddau mountains and Conwy Castle. It also benefits from having an excellent warden in Alan Davies and a wonderful team of volunteers and support staff.

As I arrived, skylarks were singing overhead despite the light rain and the banks along the edge of the footpath were a sea of yellow cowslips. Later, the warden and I led a group of birdwatchers around the reserve and saw dozens of swallows streaming up the estuary, no doubt heading further north towards their breeding grounds. In fact, the reserve is ideally placed to attract migrant birds because it's on a main flight path along the river Conwy and with a warden who's also one of Wales' best birdwatchers, rare-bird sightings are a regular occurrence. To prove the point, Alan duly found a white wagtail, a kind of pied wagtail with a grey back that passes through Wales on its way north to Iceland to breed.

I thoroughly enjoyed the day, not least because I met several youngsters who had been enthused by a pond-dipping session, one of whom confided that when she grew up, she wanted to be a wildlife reserve!

April 18th Having spent all day filming a variety of wildlife in the area around Harlech, in the evening, we accompanied a police officer called Kelvin Jones to an old barn in search of barn owls. Kelvin is an excellent birdwatcher and a great contact because, through his work, he knows every landowner in the area. He is also a very active bird-ringer and we were hoping to film him catching and ringing barn owls at a favoured breeding site.

We were not disappointed because, although the male escaped Kelvin's clutches, he successfully caught and ringed the female. Barn owls are handsome birds with their white undersides, heart-shaped face and light yellow back but their needle-sharp claws also remind you that they are perfect nocturnal killing machines and an arch-enemy of any mouse or vole unlucky enough to cross their paths. Despite a historical decline, barn owls continue to do well in many parts of rural Wales, especially those areas where vole-rich patches of rough grassland have been retained. This particular site was adjacent to a wet, species-rich grassland and it was obviously a very desirable residence for owls.

April 19th Back up to the Harlech area this morning to try to catch a polecat. We were meeting up with Kate Williamson from the Snowdonia National Park, who is studying for a PhD on the ecology of polecats. As part of her work, she sets traps for four weeks of the year in order to try to catch as many animals as possible. I had always associated polecats with farmland and woodland edges but Kate assured me that dunes were excellent places for them because they supported good populations of rabbits, their favourite prey. However, and as inevitably happens whenever a camera is brought along to capture a special moment, we failed to catch a single polecat!

BARN OWL

wild about the wild | turtles and dragons

Later in the day, we called at Barmouth to film a harbour porpoise that had been washed ashore. These small marine mammals are fairly common around the west Wales coast but these days, a worrying number are being found dead along our beaches. Up until a few years ago, the main cause of death was drowning as a result of being caught up in fishing nets but now, an increasing number are being killed by their larger relatives, the bottle-nosed dolphins.

I was astounded to learn this as I'd always been led to believe that dolphins are lovable, gentle creatures that love to frolic around our oceans. As yet, scientists are not certain why they kill porpoises but it is believed that it involves competition for an ever-declining number of fish. Whatever the reasons, it was a real shame to find such a beautiful creature washed ashore like a lump of discarded rubbish.

April 21st Yesterday, I travelled back down to the Teifi marshes to make some final preparations for a BBC wildlife series which starts next week. The weather was glorious, which probably accounts for the house martins that have suddenly appeared in good numbers and for the numerous butterflies. Peacocks were sunbathing on almost every available flower and I saw my first orange-tip of the year. The males are particularly striking with their bright white wings dipped in deep orange. One of their most important food plants is the lady's smock or cuckoo-flower and it's obviously no coincidence that this plant was in full bloom all over the wetter meadows in and around the marshes.

DEAD HARBOUR PORPOISE

iolo williams | wild about the wild

APRIL

ORANGE-TIP BUTTERFLY

The glorious weather continued into today but I found myself at the other end of Wales, on Anglesey. Newborough Forest is a large woodland which covers what was once Wales' largest sand-dune system. Today, the woodland itself is important for a variety of species and I was there to interview Dr Craig Shuttleworth who has been pivotal in ridding the forest of grey squirrels and reintroducing the native reds. Red squirrels survived on Anglesey by the skin of their teeth but now that the small population is on the increase, a handful of animals have been introduced into Newborough.

In the evening, and in the company of our enthusiastic guide Emily Dicks, we went to Llanlleiana headland, on the north coast of the island, to film porpoises feeding close offshore. We marvelled at their agility in the water, especially in such strong currents, and it was a stark contrast to the dead porpoise that had been washed ashore at Barmouth a few days earlier.

April 22nd The end of a very busy working week saw me filming at the RSPB's Inner Marsh Farm reserve on the Dee estuary. It's a wildlife haven of shallow lagoons, reed-beds and meadows that has been created from arable farmland and, over the past 20 years, it has become something of a Mecca for birdwatchers from north Wales and north-west England.

Our able guide was Colin Wells, the warden, and with the help of his sharp eyes, we were able to film dozens of different birds. We'd caught several species of ducks before they headed north for their breeding grounds whilst also catching some early migrants from further south. A small flock of whimbrel, a kind of smaller version of the curlew, had arrived from Africa and over 30 black-tailed godwits lingered in the deeper water, no doubt putting on as much weight as possible before heading north to Iceland.

On the estuary itself, I was astounded by the numbers of little egrets feeding amongst the network of creeks and had I been a few minutes earlier, I'm told I would have seen a lone avocet. I did, however, manage to see three pink-footed geese, birds that are scarce visitors to Wales these days.

On my return south, I found the time to visit the confidential site where last year, a pair of ospreys nested successfully for the first time ever in Wales. There was another pair at Porthmadog that unfortunately failed due to a succession of very wet days but the other pair managed to fledge one young. The excellent news is that the Porthmadog pair are back this year, and have been for over two weeks now. I will help to keep an eye on the 'confidential' sight over the next few weeks in the hope that those birds also return to breed.

April 23rd The boys and I headed north towards the village of Meifod in the heart of Montgomeryshire and because we had plenty of time, I decided to take the country lanes rather than the busier main road. We passed Llyn Du, a small lake about a mile from Meifod, which supports substantial numbers of coot, moorhen, mallard and tufted duck throughout the year. I remember my mother taking me there when I was about 11 years old and finding a female mallard on her nest in an old tree stump. We found no nests this time but the tree stump was still there and a pair of marsh tits ticked us off for venturing too close to their nesting tree.

A few hundred metres further on, we were startled by a flash of black closely followed by a streak of blue – a male sparrowhawk pursuing a male blackbird. The intended victim dashed into a thick hawthorn hedge but the sparrowhawk followed only for both to come flying out the other side at breakneck speed. I take my hat off to the blackbird because it then spun around, back into the hedge in the blink of an eye, whereas the hawk continued on its way through the trees to try its luck elsewhere. The whole episode had lasted no more than three explosive seconds but we'd witnessed a chase as good as any cops and robbers tale on the television.

I played rugby in the afternoon and actually managed to score a try, but my ribs took a bit of a battering and even a hot bath did little to relieve the pain.

April 24th I took a walk up the lane with the dogs in the late afternoon and visited some of the nests that I had found before heading to Indonesia two weeks ago. Two blackbird, one long-tailed tit, one robin and two song thrush nests had all failed. Of the eight nests I had previously found, only two blackbird nests now contained chicks. Most of these failures will have been caused by predation but small birds are incredibly resilient and blackbirds in particular are able to rear two, three or even four broods a year.

April 25th My final visit of the spring to film at Teifi marshes in south-west Wales proved to be very fruitful with Cetti's warbler singing like a madman as I arrived. These small, brown warblers are fairly recent colonizers of Welsh reed-beds and although they are gradually expanding northwards, numbers on the Teifi have fallen from about half a dozen pairs a few years ago to only one or two at present. The reasons for the decline remain a mystery as it looks ideal with its expanse of shrub-fringed reed-beds.

Blackcaps were also singing from the tall hedgerows and I saw my first pied flycatcher of the year – a stunning male. These are special birds of western deciduous woodlands and in many areas, populations have increased due to the provision of nest boxes. More recently, several ornithologists who monitor this species have reported widespread declines and breeding failures and it is feared that global warming may be causing its caterpillar food to emerge earlier than normal. It will take more research to discover the root of the problem, however, and I just hope that in the meantime, we can hold on to this dapper little bird in our woodlands.

The film crew and I took a canoe trip down the Teifi in the afternoon in order to film the wildlife and it's incredible how close you can get to singing chiffchaffs and willow warblers when you're on a boat. They seem unconcerned, presumably because they don't fear an unusually-shaped 'log' floating down river with on-board humans. As well as the birds, we enjoyed wonderful views of the marsh marigolds that line sections of the bank on both sides. Their flowers really are a glorious golden colour and it's no wonder that their alternative name is 'king cups'.

April 26th April is by far the best month to appreciate the plants that flower on our roadside verges and both sides of the A470 were a sea of colour as I travelled to Cardiff this morning. Cuckoo flower were particularly abundant between Llandrindod and Merthyr Tudful and it was pleasing to note that where people had mown the verges, the clouds of cuckoo flower had been left intact. Several new sections of road were lined with primroses and even cowslips were very obvious here and there.

I visited Bute Park in the centre of Cardiff to see a lesser-spotted woodpecker's nest site in a tall sycamore tree near the river Taf. These sparrow-size woodpeckers are extremely elusive, even near the nest site, and at least an hour passed before we had good views of the birds. I used to find three or four pairs around Newtown each spring but now,

I'm lucky if I find one. Whilst watching out for the woodpeckers, over a dozen swifts flew overhead, the first ones I'd seen this year, and hopefully a portent of fine weather.

The final port of call was City Hall to film an enterprising pair of ravens that has nested on the clock tower. We arrived just in time to see one of the adults flying in to feed the two newly-fledged young who were clinging onto a narrow ledge below the nest. I always associate ravens with remote mountains and isolated sea cliffs but it's wonderful to think that this charismatic bird that was once hunted to the verge of extinction is now nesting in the centre of our capital city.

April 28th Another day at Beeches' Farm alongside the River Dee near Chester and I saw my first grey partridges for over a year. These once common farmland birds now survive only where arable farmers allow wide verges and keep seed-rich stubble over the winter but it is doubtful whether any of the few remaining Welsh birds are truly wild because so many are released for shooting. I also saw the introduced red-legged or French partridge, another bird that is released onto farmland in order to be shot.

We set up two small cameras on swallow nests in some of the farm's cattle sheds and got excellent footage of the male and female visiting the

MARSH MARIGOLDS

unfinished nest with bits of straw. The structure itself is made from balls of wet mud that harden like concrete and later, straw and feathers are added to make a warm cup where the eggs will be laid. The female was becoming quite broody and twice we watched her make a deep cup by snuggling down in the straw. Twice, the male came to visit and on both occasions he was chased away by the female, so it won't be long before she begins to lay.

We attempted to film wildlife on the farm at night but unfortunately, the camera failed to pick up the animals and birds in such low light. My binoculars, however, proved to be excellent and I was able to watch hares boxing and a lone barn owl perched on a nest box erected by Steven and Anne Wrench, the farmer and his wife. On our return to the farmyard, pipistrelle bats were fluttering around the cattle sheds, feeding on the dozens of insects attracted by the bright light. When we left, it was almost midnight but Steven and Anne had to work on into the early hours as they were entering another busy lambing period.

April 29th Another day at the farm, this time in order to look for lapwing nests with a student from Bath University who has been monitoring the birds for the past two years. We found three nests with eggs in the ploughed fields and plenty of evidence of predation of eggs and even adult lapwings. From the vehicle, we were also able to pinpoint the locations of several lapwing chicks as they scurried through the furrows and rushes in search of insect food.

LAPWING NEST

It has been a long time since I last saw so many lapwing chicks together in Wales and to think that they were once so common, it is a travesty that they have disappeared from our countryside. The research undertaken on the farm shows that the 50 nesting pairs hatch the chicks fairly successfully but that precious few subsequently fledge. Small cameras on the nests have revealed that crows, foxes and badgers are the main culprits but that virtually every other predator, from stoats and weasels to kestrels and buzzards, also join in the feast.

April 30th On my early morning run along the canal, I noticed a marked difference in the plant and bird life from my last visit over a month ago. Bracken is starting to shoot up, as is the bramble and some of the tall grasses are already shading out the primroses and wood anemonies. The hedgerows, however, are still fairly devoid of leaves, and nests, usually so numerous in this particular hedge, are hard to come by.

Hissing Sid, the mute swan that terrorises walkers near the village of Aberbechan, was quite sedate this morning as his partner sheltered the unhatched eggs from the persistent drizzle. Some of the female mallards had young although the broods were very small, leading me to think that mink may have been active along this particular stretch of the canal once again. A local farmer traps the mink from time to time but it is a never-ending task, a bit like painting the Forth Bridge.

The mimicking repertoire of the male starling in the black poplar near our house is expanding almost weekly. Not only has he mastered the call of the curlew, he has now added buzzard, great spotted woodpecker and song thrush to his list. Our garden is a great place to come to learn your bird calls at the moment.

SUN, SWANS AND SNAKES

'Hissing Sid is a father at long last! As I ran past the pen on her enormous nest this morning, I could see three small, grey heads peer at me from beneath their mother's white breast feathers.'

RED CAMPION

May 1st Glorious sunshine and perfect picnic weather! So off we went to a mixed woodland on the far side of the river Severn this afternoon and tucked into our chicken legs and cheese sandwiches in the shelter of a broad oak. We were surrounded by the garlic scent of the white-flowered ramsons that grew in abundance beneath the taller trees, and in the hedgerows, primrose and wood anemone had given way to yellow archangel and red campion. It was rather sad to see the lesser celandine leaves turning anaemic and the brown, withered heads of daffodils bobbing in the breeze.

Having spent almost two hours eating, playing rugby and walking the dogs, I almost trod on a female pheasant that was incubating seven eggs within three metres of where we had been sitting. Her camouflage was perfect because none of us suspected her presence, not even the dogs. We beat a hasty retreat in the hope that the eggs would remain unmolested for her return.

May 2nd My last visit to film at Beeches' Farm on the banks of the Dee proved to be something of a mixed bag. The lapwing chicks that we had filmed a few days previously were nowhere to be seen and with the large numbers of magpies and carrion crows flying around, I didn't have to ponder long to guess what had happened to them. It may be that conservation organisations will have to bite the bullet and start employing full-time gamekeepers at sites like Beeches if the lapwing and other ground-nesting birds are to survive in Wales.

May 3rd The RSPB's South Stack reserve on the north-west tip of Anglesey is always a wonderful place to visit in spring, not only because of the wealth of wildlife but also because I am a great admirer of the people who work there. They are conservationists in the true sense of the word – committed to the birds and their habitats and not their own careers.

Today was a typical Ynys Lawd (South Stack) day with glorious sunny spells, blustery winds and, for an hour, thick sea mist. The choughs entertained the visitors by doing acrobatics on the strong breeze and the resident pair of peregrines put the fear of God into everything by putting in a brief appearance along the sea cliffs. The razorbills, guillemots and puffins are not yet back on their nesting ledges and burrows in large numbers but a sunny spell in the next week should ensure that the stragglers make their way home. The cliff tops were awash with the blues, pinks and whites of spring squill, thrift and scurvy grass and even the nationally rare and wonderfully named spatulate fleawort won't be long before its flower also puts in an appearance.

May 4th I have always avoided visiting the osprey viewing site near Porthmadog because of the plethora of politics surrounding the birds but today, I broke my duck in order to interview Kelvin Jones, one of the local volunteers who put so much effort into protecting the nesting pair when they first arrived in 2004. Despite Kelvin's hard work, and the efforts of countless volunteers, the nest collapsed in early July and the chicks fell to their death. The excellent news is that the pair has returned to a now reinforced nest and, as I learned this afternoon, the female is currently sitting on one egg with a second expected any day.

The viewing site is a good two kilometres away from the breeding pair but it has a television screen attached by microwave link to a small camera above the nest. This gives excellent views of the sitting female and you can even watch as she gets up to turn the egg or to receive a fish brought in by the male. I sincerely hope that the pair will breed successfully this year.

The politics and arguments surrounding the birds are complex, and thankfully, I have been able to keep well away from the warring parties. I don't understand why so-called conservationists can't put their differences to one side and concentrate on putting the future of the birds before their own careers, but it would appear that politics and petty jealousies are playing an ever more prominent role in Welsh conservation these days.

May 5th Moth-trapping has never been my idea of a good time but after two hours in the company of the warden at the RSPB's Ynys-hir reserve this morning, I have changed my mind. The diversity of moths we recorded was unbelievable despite the fact that the weather had been cold and drizzly but as soon as we began to inspect the light trap, the sun broke through. A moth trap works on the principle that moths are attracted to light. The trap is put out all night and is constructed so that the insects eventually fall into a receptacle beneath the light bulb itself where they can rest up without danger of predation by birds.

I don't recall the names of all the moths and to be truthful, they were all various shades of white, cream, yellow, brown and black. However, it was the complex patterns and the excellent camouflage that was so striking. One called the red sword-grass was the spitting image of a broken twig and another, called the purple thorn, looked exactly like a dead leaf. It's incredible to think that even more moths, some extremely colourful, will appear later on in the summer and I must confess that I will make every effort to go moth trapping again once the weather warms up.

May 6th Another long drive to Ynys Lawd on Anglesey, this time to try to film adders. The reserve and its acres of coastal heathland is said to be one of the best sites for this venomous snake in the whole of Wales but on dozens of previous visits, I had never seen one. To rectify this situation, we called upon the services of Wales's 'Mr Snake', Dr Rhys Jones from the University of Cardiff.

ADDER (photo: Steve Phillipps)

Within minutes of arriving, Rhys had seen the tail end of one adder disappearing into the undergrowth and a short while later, he'd found and caught one basking amongst some tall heather. She was a stunning creature with her bronze body, deep red eye and thick, black zig-zag along the length of her back. Contrary to my expectations, she was not at all aggressive and we were able to film for several minutes before returning her to the very spot where she was caught.

Adders are unfairly persecuted by man simply because they are venomous but the truth is that they bite only as a last resort. Their first instinct is to lie still and rely on their cryptic camouflage and only if threatened will they head for cover. It is when humans stand on them accidentally or try to pick them up that they strike and I have to say that if someone stood on me, I'd probably bite too.

On the way home, I drove past a delightful verge on the outskirts of Llanfair Caereinion where early purple orchids grow in abundance. They add a wonderful dash of bright purple to the whites, yellows and blues that already dapple the greens of the roadside grasses. Early purples are the commonest orchids around mid Wales and they'll grow on roadside verges, damp meadows and even on moorland edges where the land hasn't been too degraded for agriculture. Over the next few weeks, I can expect to come across many more species but as they hybridize freely, it isn't always easy to distinguish one from another.

May 7th Hissing Sid is a father at long last! As I ran past the pen on her enormous nest this morning, I could see three small, grey heads peer at me from beneath their mother's white breast feathers. Sid was standing guard, as always, and is obviously taking fatherhood as seriously as ever because the dogs and I were escorted out of his territory. In fact, he swam with his chest stuck out for almost half a kilometre before he was happy that we posed no threat to his newborn. No doubt some poor walker will feel the wrath of Sid's powerful wings over the coming weeks.

The natural vegetation of the riverbank is slowly sinking under the green canopy of alien species once more. Giant hogweed, Japanese knotweed and Himalayan balsam are all growing rapidly and shading out the lesser celandines and garlic mustard that were so obvious two weeks ago. The giant hogweed is a dangerous plant as chemicals in the sap will react with sunlight once in contact with the skin to cause severe blistering. Last year, two canal workers who were strimming the banks had to take a few weeks off work because so much sap had come into contact with their skin. I don't believe we will find a way to eradicate these invasive aliens in the near future, if ever, so we'll just have to accept them as a natural part of our flora.

May 9th On my run along the canal in bright sunshine, I met Sid, his mate and five cygnets out for a morning swim. Sid looked the archetypal proud parent as he led the way along the water and he was even willing to allow the dogs and myself to have a quick glimpse of his new family before reverting back to type and hissing at us until we moved on. The

iolo williams | wild about the wild

HISSING SID, HIS WIFE AND THEIR CYGNETS!

next few months will be a dangerous time for the youngsters and they'll do well to stay close to their parents for protection against mink, foxes and a host of other threats.

Today was our last visit to the RSPB reserve at Ynys-hir on the Dyfi estuary and what a glorious evening it turned out to be. The sun shone throughout the latter part of the day although the north-westerly wind was bitingly cold. Whilst filming along a woodland boardwalk, I found a jay sitting low down in its nest in the fork of a gnarled birch tree. It was partly hidden by ivy but I could just make out the bird's beak and tail with a large eye staring straight into my binoculars. Jay nests are usually well-hidden but this one was one of the most obvious I've ever come across. It's certainly safe from the clutches of man but whether other predators will find it remains to be seen.

Further up the river Dyfi, we watched a pair of little egrets fly to and from their nest in amongst a large heronry. This beautiful, snow-white heron has increased dramatically in recent years and although it nested on the south coast of England for the first time in the early 1990s, only in recent years has it nested in Wales. Now, however, small groups can be seen on virtually every Welsh estuary and it won't be long before they are nesting in every county.

I saw my first whinchat of the year in the beautiful evening light as flocks of swifts screamed overhead. It really was a wonderful way to say goodbye to a magnificent reserve.

May 10th Whilst filming at Roath Park in the centre of Cardiff, I watched two great crested grebes fighting over a mate. I had previously seen pairs undertaking the complex mating 'dance' for which this species is so famous, but I had never seen them fight with such ferocity before. One bird held the other under the water whilst appearing to force its beak open. The 'drowning' bird struggled to keep any part of its body, let alone its head, above water for any length of time and I was certain that it had drowned. After several minutes, however, it managed to wrestle free from its opponent's grip and escape. Meanwhile, the watching female decided that she liked the loser and went off after him, leaving the dominant male to wonder what he'd done wrong.

May 11th Dr Fred Slater is another one of Wales's gem naturalists who knows a lot about virtually everything and is excellent at expressing himself on camera or on the radio. The last time I spoke to him, we were discussing frogs and toads but at the University of Wales's Llysdinam Field Centre this morning, we were looking at newts.

The pond at the centre is full of amphibians and now holds all three species of British newt. The largest and most impressive is the protected great crested newt that can grow up to 16 centimetres in length. It has a black body and a fiery-orange belly with dark patterns, each individual having a pattern as unique as a fingerprint. The smooth newt is much smaller and lighter and has dark spots on its underside, including the throat. The smallest member of the family is the palmate newt and breeding males of this species have dark hind feet and thin black filament on the end of the tail.

Newts are fascinating creatures that spend most of their lives under logs or in tall, damp vegetation before emerging in April and early May to lay their single eggs on aquatic vegetation. Most garden ponds will contain newts although, because they are mainly nocturnal, they can often go unnoticed by the owners.

In the evening, we travelled down to Tal-y-Bont on Usk Youth Hostel to trap bats in the company of Phil Morgan, one of Wales's foremost mammal experts. Phil monitors several species of bats but this evening, he was catching midge pipistrelle bats as they appeared from their daytime roost in the eaves of an old building. They are very dog-like in appearance and it was fascinating to see just how thin the wing is. Basically, it's a layer of skin that has been stretched out over elongated finger bones but it is extremely effective and allows bats to take advantage of the thousands of insects that fly around after dark.

It is said that one pipistrelle can eat 3,000 midges in a night. As we were bitten to death by midges whilst waiting for the bats to emerge, I did consider taking a handful of bats with me wherever I go but they are a protected species and Phil had to have a licence to handle them. In all, over 200 bats emerged from the roost but later in the summer, they could number over 1,000. They'll need an awful lot of midges.

May 12th We filmed around the Elan valley all day today, concentrating on the ancient woodlands and their wildlife in the company of Ray Woods of the Countryside Council for Wales. Ray makes botany interesting with his endless facts and figures and I was surprised to learn that our old trees support somewhere in the region of 1,300 species of beetles. If you add to that the thousands of other insects, birds, fungi and other plants and animals, the figures are absolutely mind-blowing.

May 13th Although I was born in Builth Wells, we moved away when I was only a few months old and I never get the opportunity to walk around the town these days. This morning, however, I had half an hour to spare before moving south to Erwood and I walked the dogs along a lovely path along the banks of the river Irfon where it flows into the Wye.

With me, once more, was Ray Woods and he opened my eyes to the number of introduced plants around us. I knew that the 'big three', namely Japanese knotweed, Himalayan balsam and giant hogweed were not only alien, but also destructive, and I also knew that the sycamore is an introduced species. Beneath my feet, however, Ray showed me a small plant with a beautiful blue flower called 'sin', presumably because it is a forbidden species that reproduces freely, and Spanish bluebells.

The latter is a garden escapee that is hybridizing with our native bluebell in many areas and when you consider how unique our bluebell woods are in world terms, this could be an environmental disaster in the making. Beautiful though they are, Spanish bluebells belong in Spain and it's up to all gardeners to ensure that they don't throw bulbs from this invasive species onto compost heaps or into rivers.

May 15th Hedgehogs have suddenly appeared over the past two weeks or so, not that I've seen a live one as yet, but I have come across several killed on the roads of mid Wales. They are far scarcer than they were when I was a teenager when we regularly saw them as we walked across fields and gardens at night. These days, I rarely see a living one apart from the few scurrying to escape my car headlights. Later in the year, I will put out wood piles and some dry bedding around the edges of the garden in the hope of encouraging them to hibernate.

May 16th On the way to Anglesey again, I saw my first stoat of the year. It ran across the road a few metres in front of the car near the village of Llanerfyl in north Montgomeryshire and had I blinked, I would have missed it completely. Stoats are larger than weasels with a black tip to the tail and I always think of the latter as a sausage with legs and the former as a frankfurter with legs. Wait until the next time you see one and you'll know exactly what I mean.

I don't see either species very often these days but I remember as a youth attracting a whole family of stoats out of dense cover by making squealing noises. They are very inquisitive and as long as you stay completely still, you can sometimes entice them to come to within a few metres. Gamekeepers used to use this to their advantage in the olden days and I remember one old keeper telling me how he'd managed to get a stoat to come right up to the barrel of his gun before he shot it!

The verges of the A55 along the north Wales coast are stunning at the moment with thousands of ox-eye daisies bobbing their large white and yellow heads in the breeze stirred by passing vehicles. The cowslips that were so prominent a few days ago have died back to be replaced by red campion and bird's-foot trefoil although the gorse still looks magnificent in its coconut-scented yellow cloak.

May 18th Yesterday was one of those occasions when I question just how green I really am. I recycle everything I possibly can, I turn lights off whenever I leave the room and I rarely put the heating on in the house because it has been so well insulated but yesterday, I drove four hours down to Devon and four hours back just for a four-minute interview with Bill Oddie. It was a pleasant ride and Bill was, as ever, great company, but the four-hour return journey gave me plenty of time to question my commitment to the environment.

Today was a day off. But I felt so guilty about not working that I called by an old friend from RSPB days to do a radio interview. Roger Lovegrove was head of the RSPB in Wales for more than 25 years until his retirement in the late 1990s and it was a role that he filled with great ability and enthusiasm. He is one of Welsh conservation's more charismatic figures and it's sad to see that a lot of the senior managerial posts in the RSPB today seem to have been filled by colourless individuals.

After the interview, we walked around Roger's garden and I was amazed to find more than a dozen species nesting within a relatively

GORSE

small area. Pied flycatchers and great tits had commandeered his nest boxes, blackcaps and garden warblers had built homes in the tangles of bushes and brambles, a goldfinch had constructed its cup nest in a climbing rose and, most remarkable of all, pied and grey wagtails were sitting on eggs within a few centimetres of each other in the same bush.

May 19th On the bracken-covered slopes of the Elan valley, tree pipits had arrived back on their breeding grounds in substantial numbers and I watched several males participating in simultaneous parachute-display flights where they descend from the heavens with wings half open, singing constantly. They are a warmer creamy colour than meadow pipits and can often be seen singing from a prominent hawthorn or rowan tree amongst the bracken. Another migrant singing to the best of its capabilities was the whinchat, the lovely orange, brown and white male alarm-calling as I neared the hidden nest site.

In late afternoon, we travelled the short distance to the red kite feeding station at Gigrin Farm on the outskirts of Rhaeadr. To anyone who hasn't been there, you are missing a wildlife spectacle that rivals anything Britain has to offer as up to 400 kites come down to feed on meat put out

PIED FLYCATCHER

by Chris Powell, the farmer. The kites battle it out with the local ravens, buzzards, crows and herons for the tastiest morsels, often indulging in prolonged and noisy aerial battles. Even on a quiet mid-week afternoon in the middle of May, over 150 people had crammed into the hides placed adjacent to the feeding site and not a single person left for home disappointed.

BLUEBELLS

As a footnote to the Gigrin Farm visit, I must mention the world's bravest animal. As we watched about 200 red kites, 50 ravens, 10 buzzards, 2 herons and over 100 crows spiralling around each other in a feeding frenzy, a young rabbit hopped out of some rushes into the middle of the battlefield, apparently oblivious to everything and everyone around her. Much to the amazement of all of us watching, she grazed happily and unmolested for over ten minutes before disappearing once more into the tangle of tall vegetation. That individual should be mentioned in rabbit despatches come the day of reckoning.

May 22nd Today, Ceri and I took the boys down to the Elan valley to escape the rain that had kept us indoors for most of yesterday.

The boys built a dam across a clear mountain stream whilst I walked the dogs along one of the many forest walks. The bluebells were at their best beneath the gnarled old oaks and when the sun came out, speckled wood and orange-tip butterflies flew along the forest rides in search of nectar. I sat amongst the carpet of flowers on the woodland floor to watch and listen and unbeknown to the dogs sleeping by my side, a cock pheasant sneaked up to within a few metres of our position. He was a stunning, purple-green colour with bright red cheeks, although I was unable to get a good look at him because he was unwilling to risk coming out into the open.

Back at the stream, a major construction was underway as the wood and stone dam neared completion. The boys would take a break every few minutes in order to inspect a particularly large earthworm or centipede they had found, then carried on with the task in hand once more. I had done exactly the same with my brother in the streams around Llanwddyn over 30 years ago and I hope my grandchildren and their grandchildren will be doing the same thing in years to come.

May 23rd Newtown is a great place to watch swifts in the summer months and after taking the boys to school this morning, I parked the car to watch them screaming overhead as parties of half a dozen and more raced up and down Broad Street. They nest under the eaves of some of the older buildings and although they are one of the last migrants to arrive on our shores, they are also one of the first to leave. Called 'devil birds' by some, they were the favourite birds of a colleague of mine from RSPB days who died of cancer last year and I can't think of swifts without thinking about her.

Hissing Sid and his partner have walked their five cygnets the short distance from the Montgomeryshire canal to the river Severn. Here, they'll find a greater variety of food and better places to roost because in the past, Sid's offspring have been vulnerable to fox and mink predation on the canal. It will be interesting to see how the chicks fare on the river as last year's brood stayed on the canal and all five survived until the spring. One thing's for sure, they couldn't ask for a more attentive and protective father.

May 24th I'm obviously not the only one who admires the clouds of swifts flying over the old streets of Newtown. When I called by the post office this afternoon, my eye was suddenly drawn to a dark, scythe-shaped form cutting repeatedly through the flocks of swift, spreading panic through every small bird in the sky. It was a hobby, not long arrived back from Africa and trying its very best to catch its afternoon meal.

It flew so low overhead that I was able to make out its black moustache and orange-red 'socks' but despite its best efforts, the swifts remained out of harm's way. Their panic was well founded because hobbies are one of the few birds agile and fast enough to catch swifts, martins and swallows on the wing, but eventually this individual decided to give up the ghost and look elsewhere for its food. I must have watched it flying for about 30 seconds above a packed street but no one else looked skywards during that whole time.

May 26th I'm extremely fortunate with my work in that I love what I do. I'm also lucky to be able to mix my television presenting with a smattering of radio programmes in both languages, all of them dealing with wildlife. Today, I was doing an interview at Dolanog in north Montgomeryshire for a half-hour programme on butterflies.

To be fair to Simon Spencer, mid Wales's butterfly expert, it wasn't the ideal day to see these beautiful insects because they love sunshine and in cold, cloudy weather, they stay put. Allt Dolanog is an area of bracken-covered hill which is ideal for many species of butterflies, particularly the fritillaries. In fact, it is the only site in Wales that supports five species of fritillaries, butterflies that are now declining throughout their British range. The rarest of these, the high brown fritillary, is now confined to two sites in Wales and the one we were searching for, the pearl-bordered fritillary, survives in fewer than a dozen.

Only 25 years ago, most of the fritillaries were species with a widespread Welsh distribution but habitat loss, as with so much of our wildlife, caused rapid declines. Thankfully, the commoners at Dolanog are pleased to have their rare butterflies and now lightly graze the bracken slopes for most of the year. This encourages violets, the fritillary caterpillars' favourite plant, as well as a variety of other flowers that provide nectar for the adults.

We didn't see a single fritillary, however! Never mind: Simon's company was stimulating and, even without the butterflies, Allt Dolanog remains a special place.

May 27th Down to Cardiff for the last day's filming on the *Welsh Safari* series and a chance to meet up with Rhys 'Snake Man' Jones again. On the journey down, I noticed how several flowers, including foxgloves, were flowering much earlier south of the Brecon Beacons because of the warmer weather. It was also nice to see a red kite circling above the road only 15 miles from the centre of Cardiff. It's only a matter of time before they start nesting on the edges of our capital city and they may eventually scavenge the streets once more, like they used to do in large towns during the Middle Ages.

Rhys and I went looking for grass snakes around Llys-faen reservoir, north of Cardiff. It's ideal habitat because it consists of a lake full of frogs and toads, damp meadows full of mice and voles, and plenty of warm, south-facing banks. The fact that we'd chosen the hottest day of the year so far certainly helped Rhys to find a metre-long female grass snake and the first thing she did was secrete the contents of her anal gland over his hands. He stank to high heaven but he explained that this was a defence mechanism because the stench, allied to the fact that she would pretend to be dead if attacked by a predator, gave the impression that her corpse was rotten.

I haven't seen a grass snake for four years and it was a rare treat to be able to inspect such a creature at close quarters. She was far more active than the adder Rhys had shown me at Ynys Lawd a few weeks earlier and that's because, once warmed by the sun's rays, she'll move through the grass and adjacent ponds in search of her prey. Adders, on the other hand, are ambush predators, lying in wait for a vole or lizard to pass within striking distance.

GRASS SNAKE

Once we'd finished filming, we released the snake where we found her, then stumbled across another one, this time a monster of about a metre and a half in length. When picked up, she immediately acted as if she was dead with her eyes closed and her tongue hanging limply out of her mouth. When released, however, she showed an amazing turn of speed to escape into the tall grass. All in all, an excellent day and one that was finished in style with a few beers in the Cardiff hot-spots.

May 29th I love visiting Pembrokeshire, but I hate the coast road between Aberystwyth and Cardigan during the summer months because of the volume of traffic, especially caravans and lorries. Still, the occasional kite and chough breaks up the journey nicely.

I was making my way to Dale to launch a new marine code of conduct for boat owners and part of the deal was that we were taken out into St Bride's Bay and around Skomer Island. For those of you who have never been to the island, you have missed out on a real treat. It supports over 100,000 pairs of Manx shearwaters as well as thousands of puffins, guillemots and razorbills. In May, the island itself is coated in a carpet of red and blue – campion and bluebells – with a few thousand gulls dotted here and there.

As we approached open water, we watched hundreds of gannets from nearby Grassholm plunging into the sea after mackerel, no doubt drawn to the exact spot by the numerous harbour porpoises that were also oblivious to our boat while they fished. Pembrokeshire is so well blessed with coastal wildlife that a marine code of conduct is essential, especially when you consider the volume of tourists now attracted to many of the seabird and cetacean hot-spots. Later in the year, boats will also take tourists out to see grey seals giving birth on remote beaches, so the potential for disturbance is enormous. Luckily, most boat owners are very sensitive to the wildlife and any rogues will now be dealt with appropriately.

On the way back, I made a small detour to visit the display set up by a small charity called Sea Watch at the marine centre in Fishguard. Under the auspices of an excellent local naturalist called Cliff Benson, this organisation maps the numbers and distribution of cetaceans and other marine wildlife around the south-west Wales coast. I must make time to go out with them on one of their counts because, by all accounts, they see some incredible wildlife including basking sharks and sunfish, two huge marine fish.

wild about the wild | sun, swans and snakes

May 30th A lovely, sunny day yet again! On the way home from a picnic in the grounds of Gregynog Hall, a weasel crossed the road in front of the car, the first one I've seen this year. It disappeared into a particularly well-vegetated roadside verge and try as I might, I could not tempt it back out into the open by making squealing noises.

There was time in the evening to go for a run along the canal and find that Hissing Sid, his pen and all five cygnets have now moved back to the canal from the adjacent river Severn. The scourge of the ramblers is back!

COMMON SANDPIPER NEST

May 31st Every spring, I promise myself that I will leave as many free days as I possibly can to explore the woods and hills that I walked as a boy and every spring, the end of May arrives before I can blink. What happened to those school holidays that lasted months and the never-ending Bank Holiday weekends of my childhood? These days, a month is no more than a long weekend and a year passes in a week.

At least I was able to pass on some childhood wisdom to my two boys this morning when I showed them some of the plants they could eat if they were hungry. One of the nicest and easiest to identify is pig nut, an umbellifer from the same family as the cow parsley that has an edible tuber. The boys had great fun digging these up but they weren't quite so keen to eat them, knowing that home and a packet of crisps were only ten minutes away. I found them delicious, as were the leaves of the wood sorrel carpeting the floor of a nearby conifer plantation, and even the boys nibbled at these.

It was such a warm day, we all dived into the river after our feast and scared the life out of a common sandpiper that was incubating four eggs on a well-vegetated island. Having arrived in April, this was probably a second attempt at nesting after the first had failed because they rear only one brood a year. The incubating bird flew to the bank calling constantly until we swam away but it took some minutes before she returned to her eggs and only then after she'd flown around the area a few times to make sure there were no predators lying in wait.

All in all, it was a wonderful way to end the month but the weatherman says that there's rain on the way.

MAD DOGS AND MERLINS

'Today, the sunshine arrived with a vengeance! By the afternoon, it was a sizzling 29° Celsius and the dogs went on strike, escaping the heat by lying on the cool, wooden floor of the hall.'

Dog Rose

June 1st The weatherman was correct. It poured down with rain all morning! But this did not stop me travelling to the Cwmaman Institute to open an Environmental Film Festival this afternoon. It's not often I get to visit a new area within Wales so I was delighted to encounter this lovely and forgotten part of the country.

On the way to Cwmaman, I passed some excellent *ffridd*-covered slopes full of yellowhammers, tree pipits, cuckoos and green woodpeckers, all birds that have virtually gone from many other parts of Wales. The area's rivers once more support fish such as brown trout and salmon which feed on the abundance of insects and these have brought with them birds and mammals such as dippers, kingfishers and otters. Those post-industrial south Wales valleys, so often stigmatized environmentally, are alive and well and, from a wildlife point of view, doing very nicely, thank you.

June 2nd I'm filming a one-hour programme on the red kite for S4C this year and today, we filmed a nest in an oak woodland not too far from Aberystwyth. The two chicks are well-grown by now and can withstand virtually anything nature can throw at them, which is just as well because we had some fairly heavy showers around midday. By now, both parents leave them for long periods so that they can search for food although this pair is fortunate in that the kite feeding station at Nant-yr-arian is not too far away.

The nest itself is typical red kite. It's a mass of sticks placed in the fork of a stunted sessile oak and lined with sheep's wool. By this late stage, the nest rim is dotted with the remains of rabbits, magpies and carrion crows that are either picked up dead or caught as inexperienced youngsters and, on a hot day, hundreds of bluebottles gather to feast on the rotting remains. Indeed, in the past I have found some nests by smell, such was the stench of putrefying flesh.

We then moved on to Nantyrarian itself to watch the kites being fed and it was heartening to see so many visitors on such a miserable day. They watched mesmerised as the kites circled, waiting for their lunch, and then I heard a loud 'aaah' as the first half dozen birds swooped down for the meat. Ceredig, the man who runs the feeding station, told me that over the years, the kites have become increasingly bold and two weeks previously, he was accidentally struck on the head by a kite coming down to feed. This from a bird that, until a few years ago, immediately retreated at the sight of man following three centuries of persecution.

June 5th I've insisted that the County Council does not mow the roadside verges that abut our garden and now, I'm glad that I did. The sea of cow parsley and red campion is about to be joined by hundreds of meadowsweet flowers and whereas the verges around the village itself are a monotone of short turf, the diversity up here is incredible. Once the sun comes out, the buzzing of the wasps, bees and hoverflies can be deafening for several metres and a song thrush spends many hours searching for snails among the base of the taller plants before battering them on its stone anvil near the gatepost.

June 6th I recently bought a new zoom lens to go with my digital camera and it has opened up a whole new world for me. I now take it with me everywhere and I keep my eyes open for any potential photograph, be it a butterfly sunning itself, a cluster of beautiful flowers or a bird tugging an earthworm from the ground. I'm not saying that I'm any good at it yet, but I'm trying.

BANDED DEMOISELLE

June 7th Last night, I spent a very pleasant evening at the Chain Bridge Hotel overlooking the river Dee outside Llangollen. The hotel is superbly located and allows you to eat your evening meal whilst looking out at the river and its wildlife. We saw a female goosander with her punk haircut guiding five youngsters through a maze of rapids. One was quite nervous about the whole ordeal and kept trying to go overland only to be scolded by mother for hanging back. Eventually, they all made it through safely to a shallow pool where the mother appeared to herd small fish towards her offspring so that they could dive after them. After several unsuccessful attempts, one of the chicks eventually came up with a fish in its beak and a triumphant look on its face.

We watched at least two pairs of grey wagtails dashing to and fro in pursuit of insects and a lone dipper dashed underwater to search for invertebrates between the submerged rocks. The undoubted highlight, however, was a flash of blue and orange that lasted no more than a few seconds – a kingfisher on its way to fish in calmer waters.

Today was the first real hint of summer as the temperatures soared under a clear blue sky. We filmed on a longboat crossing the Froncysyllte aqueduct, a superb feat of engineering when you consider that it was built by Thomas Telford exactly 200 years ago. It's an odd experience being on a longboat that's suspended 120 feet up in the air looking down at the Dee valley. I was able to watch jackdaws and buzzards circle beneath me as we floated quietly overhead. It's probably an even stranger experience for the birds!

June 9th Travelling by longboat on a canal is an excellent way to unwind and to watch wildlife. You encounter all kinds of plants and animals that would be difficult to see whilst walking and because the boats are so quiet, you don't disturb them as you would in a car. Yesterday, whilst travelling from Chirk to Ellesmere, I watched a garden warbler feeding her young in a nest tucked into a tussock of grass in the canal bank. The parent was met by four wide, yellow gapes all begging for the juicy morsels it was carrying in its beak. One false move for these chicks and they would end up in the canal but at least they were safe from foxes, stoats and weasels.

On the way to Whitchurch, we stopped briefly at Fenn's and Whixall Moss, a weird area on the Welsh border that resembles the boggy flatlands of Norfolk and Lincolnshire. It's a haven for wildlife, supporting 27 species of dragonfly, the rare large heath butterfly and birds such as curlew, cuckoo, skylark and yellowhammer. While we were filming, several curlew could be heard calling in the distance and it reminded me of the wet fields around Llanwddyn when I was a wild about the wild | mad dogs and merlins

young lad, wet fields that have long since disappeared. Thankfully, the mosses are now in the safe hands of English Nature and the Countryside Council for Wales and work to restore them to their former glory is continuing.

June 10th My dad's 83rd birthday. He grew up on a farm in the hills above Cwm-twrch in the upper Swansea valley and then, soon after returning from the war, he decided to go into teaching. All his life, he has been a true gentleman, treating people and animals as he would wish to be treated himself. I have the utmost respect for him.

I phoned him to wish him a happy birthday from the mere that has given the town of Ellesmere its name. It's a great place to watch wildlife that may not be rare but that is generally quite shy and retiring. I watched a great crested grebe on its nest, a pair of coots with their six yellow and red-headed youngsters and a dozen young swans gliding gracefully through the water before being chased away by the resident male.

COOT ON NEST

Coots are particularly numerous on the mere because the well-vegetated shallows provide it with ample feeding and nesting sites. They are extremely aggressive towards each other and it was comical to watch two birds from neighbouring pairs threatening each other by swimming towards one another with their heads down and bottoms raised. Invariably, such disputes result in a full-blown fight and sometimes, the incubating bird will fly off the nest to join its mate. They have sharp claws on the ends of their partially webbed feet and these can inflict some considerable damage on an opponent.

June 11th I saw very little wildlife on my early morning run in the drizzle but by late afternoon, the weather had improved and I decided to walk the dogs along the river Severn near Aber-miwl. It's a well-trodden path and to be honest, I wasn't expecting to see anything out of the ordinary but, as ever, wildlife has a way of surprising you when you least expect it.

A common sandpiper dashed silently from a well-vegetated part of the shingle. Generally, they are very noisy birds but this one kept as quiet as a mouse and merely flew out of view behind some reed canary grass about 50 metres further downstream. I walked on carefully and eventually found a small depression containing four well-marked eggs at the base of a tall sorrel. The sandpiper was nesting in an area that was well frequented by dog walkers and with so many potential hazards around, her defence was to sneak away quietly and hope that the camouflaged eggs would not be found. If the eggs hatch, I would expect her to lead the chicks to a less disturbed part of the riverbank.

June 12th I took my sons to north Wales to see Taid and Nain and on the way, we saw at least three tawny owl road-kills. At this time of year, the newly-fledged young are on the wing and therefore very vulnerable to being struck by passing traffic. I often come across owls perched in the middle of the road at night, dazzled by my car headlights and it is only by stopping, putting the lights off and hooting my horn that I get them to fly away.

Talking of owls, last night I went outside to look for a hedgehog in the garden and I heard our resident tawny owl chicks calling from the direction of a large Scots pine over the way. At least two chicks have fledged but I didn't want to go over to look for them as the adult female has been known to attack people in the past. She is, of course, merely defending her offspring and her actions are to be admired. By the way, the rustling I'd heard at the base of the garden hedge turned out not to be a hedgehog but a large toad.

After seeing my parents, I called into the osprey-viewing site near Porthmadog on my return journey to find that two of the three eggs have hatched, the second one at one o'clock this afternoon. Let's hope there's enough food in the surrounding rivers, lakes and estuaries to feed both chicks. If the third egg also hatches, it will be a minor miracle for all three young to survive to fledging but with all the media attention on this pair, we shall no doubt have weekly updates via the television and radio.

June 13th I spent the day in and around Llanelli, recording some radio interviews at the Penclacwydd Wildfowl and Wetlands Centre. As well as the impressive collection of exotic wildfowl, they also have some excellent habitats for our native wildlife, including some damp pastures full of ragged robin. This plant has lovely, dark pink flowers that resemble those of a red campion whose petals have been flailed, hence the name ragged robin. I remember it as a fairly common plant of damp meadows but as the land has been drained, this beautiful flower has become more scarce.

Many of the roadside verges around the centre are full of southern marsh orchids at present and where these were sheltered by hazel and hawthorn hedges, speckled wood butterflies could be seen fluttering in

SPECKLED WOOD BUTTERFLY

the sunlight. These are amazing insects that defend their own small territories against other large insects and when several speckled woods come together, they circle around each other in a dizzy spiral. One of them chased away a brimstone butterfly that had the audacity to land on a cluster of red campion. The brimstone has leaf-like wings that allow it to hang unseen under bushes during cold and damp weather conditions or overnight and it's likely that its yellow colouring gave rise to the term 'butter coloured fly' that was later shortened to butterfly.

June 14th This was another one of those memorable days spent in the field with two ornithologists that I greatly respect. I met Tony Cross of the Welsh Kite Trust and Brian Jones, a kite warden, in the small village of Llangamarch before going on to four confidential sites to ring the kite chicks. Being able to watch such wonderful birds at close quarters is a rare privilege, especially as I used to warden kites during my days with

BARN OWL CHICK

the RSPB. It was heartening to hear that we now have about 500 breeding pairs in Wales, a staggering increase from the 40 or so pairs in the country when I first became involved in red kite conservation back in the early 1980s.

Tony is an excellent tree climber and he would scale the large oaks and sycamores in record time so that he and Brian could ring and tag the juveniles. This is important work because we learn so much about the birds' movements and survival rates without harming them in any way. In fact, kite chicks lie as if dead when they are being ringed, unlike smaller birds of prey such as sparrowhawks and kestrels that rip your hands to shreds given half a chance. In all, we visited four nests and ringed three chicks. Unfortunately, one nest had failed. The prey list for the final nest was particularly impressive as it featured several members of the crow family, including magpies, rooks, carrion crows and a jay, all caught either in the nest or as recently fledged youngsters.

On the way between kite nests, Brian took us to a derelict barn where he and Tony proceeded to ring four barn owl chicks. Two were found on the floor beneath the nest and were badly undernourished but it is hoped that now they are back in the box, they will thrive once more. Barn owls are one of our most attractive birds and although I wasn't

RED KITE CHICK

allowed near the nest because I do not hold a licence to monitor this species, I watched from afar as one of the adults glided silently out of a loft window and into a nearby tree. Elsewhere in Britain, these owls appear to be fairly scarce but in most areas of Wales, they are now holding their own after a long period of decline.

To cap an excellent day, at the last kite nest, we met the farmer, Brian Watkins, who turned out to be a mine of information on the Abergwesyn area and its birds. He told me that he had gone with his father to see red kites in the upper Tywi valley in 1947 and that they had first appeared in the Irfon valley in about 1952. Despite having watched them from afar for five decades, they had never nested on his land until this year and the look of pride on his face as he watched 'his' chick being ringed was something to behold. There is no doubt that without the cooperation of farmers such as Brian, kites would have died out in Britain during the last century. Our debt to them is a huge one.

June 15th Two miserable days of low cloud and drizzle haven't replenished the water supplies of Welsh rivers and lakes but it's certainly brought the song thrushes and blackbirds into the garden. The wet weather has caused thousands of snails to become active so our resident song thrushes are feeding to their hearts' content and using one of our flagstones as an anvil.

Over the past few days, fruits have suddenly appeared on many of the trees where flowers were formerly present. Next door's apple trees have lost all their blossom and small, young apples have appeared almost overnight. My small Bardsey apple tree may produce some fruits this year, if I can beat the blackbirds and wasps to it, but even if I lose the race, I'll have the satisfaction of knowing that something has been fed by a tree that I planted as a sapling only 18 months ago. Down the lane, all the horse chestnut blossom that was blown away by high winds two weeks ago has now been replaced by hundreds of miniature, spiny green cases. It's a sobering thought that in only a few months, the boys and I will be out once more in search of fresh, reddish-brown conkers.

June 17th Today, I headed to north Wales to record several radio interviews, the first at the National Trust's Craflwyn centre near Beddgelert with warden Dave Smith. One of his constant battles over the years has been to try to eradicate rhododendron from Nant Gwynant and it would appear, after spending hundreds of thousands of pounds, that the war is being won. They have now cleared whole hillsides of this introduced pest and it was wonderful to see native plants returning to sites that they had not occupied for over a century. Genetic analysis has shown that our 'feral' rhododendron comes from the Iberian peninsula where, ironically, it is now a threatened species. They are more than welcome to the thousands of hectares of Snowdonia rhododendron.

My next interview was with Plantlife's Wales officer, Trevor Dines. One of our best botanists, Trevor also has infectious enthusiasm for his work and he managed to put introduced plants into a proper perspective. Over half of our flora are alien species but it is only a handful that hit the headlines as destructive pests. Many were introduced with the move from human hunter-gatherers to farmers some 8,000 years ago and with market gardening such big business at present, several more are sure to follow. There's no doubting the fact that without alien species, such as the beautiful, red common poppy, our countryside would be a far less interesting place to walk.

June 18th Today, the sunshine arrived with a vengeance! By the afternoon, it was a sizzling 29° Celsius and the dogs went on strike, escaping the heat by lying on the cool, wooden floor of the hall. The only sound was the buzzing of flies and the occasional bleating lamb and it was as if the whole of the natural world was taking a siesta. Everyone, that is, except my two boys who insisted that dad joined them for a game of rugby. Mad dogs and Welshmen . . .

June 19th Another hot and humid day and yet another visit to the banks of the Severn with the family. The common sandpiper was off her nest, probably disturbed by a picnicking family and their two dogs. The eggs should survive as long as they are not located by a passing predator – they certainly won't chill on a day like today.

We walked along the canal in the afternoon where Sid the swan and his partner are moulting their flight feathers. I've started a nature table at the Welsh school in Newtown so the boys and I thought it would be good to add some very special swan feathers to the collection. Like us, the good people of Aberbechan take great pride in the fact that they have the world's fiercest swan on their doorstep.

In the late evening, I travelled to Anglesey for an early start the following morning and as I arrived on the island, a thin layer of mist was just appearing over the fields. As I crossed Malltraeth Marsh, I could see the yellow heads of flag irises peeping over the creeping mist like a scene from a horror film and just before arriving at Rhoscolyn, a barn owl glided across the road in front of the car.

June 21st We spent two glorious days filming around Mynydd Twr, near Holyhead and Ynys Lawd (South Stack) in bright sunshine. Much of the first day was spent in the Breakwater Reserve on the outskirts of Holyhead itself and it appeared as if every bush had its own pair of whitethroat or stonechat. In Wales, both of these birds have a strongly coastal distribution where the mixture of gorse, low bushes, tall vegetation and mild weather provide an ideal habitat.

Two years ago, over half of Mynydd Twr had gone up in smoke and, because the soil is shallow, nearly all the plants and animals were killed outright. Nature has a wonderful way of reclaiming lost land, however, and new heather shoots were springing up everywhere along with thousands of heath spotted orchids in their various shades of pinks and purples. We searched for adders but to no avail, probably because the vegetation was not yet tall enough to hide them.

Ynys Lawd was its usual wonderful self with its sea of red campion, carpets of thrift and thousands of beautiful, blue sheep's-bit scabious. The seabirds drew most of the crowds, with over 4,500 pairs of guillemots, almost a thousand razorbills and a handful of puffins crammed onto the cliffs. The first two are superbly well-adapted to life on the cliffs because they lay triangular-shaped eggs. This means that when one is accidentally knocked, it spins around itself rather than roll off the narrow ledge. Within two weeks, the thousands of chicks will have launched themselves off the precipitous cliffs into the sea and the seabird citadel will fall silent once more.

June 22nd When I worked for the RSPB, one of my favourite tasks was to monitor breeding hen harriers and merlin on the Berwyn moors. Today, I had a chance to retrace some of my steps in the company of Keith Offord who works for the Countryside Council for Wales. Keith knows the moors well having worked on them intermittently for almost 30 years and I was invited to accompany him as he undertook his last visit to some traditional harrier breeding sites.

Hen harriers are magical birds and I remember as if it were yesterday the first time I found a pair breeding on the moors above Llyn Efyrnwy. That was way back in 1974 and I have returned to the moors every year

wild about the wild | mad dogs and merlins

MERLIN CHICKS

since but in recent times, a busy work schedule has meant that most visits have been very fleeting. Today was different because Keith and I had all day to catch up on old times and watch these spectacular birds of prey on their breeding grounds.

There is nothing quite like the sight of a ghostly-grey male hen harrier floating silently over the heather with prey in its talons for the female. He then whistles gently until she flies up off her nest and flips beneath him to take the food in a manoeuvre known as a food pass. Today, I watched not one but three food passes at two different sites and to add to the enjoyment, we were also able to watch a pair of merlins near the nest. These are small, fast-flying falcons and whereas the harrier food pass is a rather gentle affair, the female merlin is rather more forthright. The male, like the harrier, calls the female off the nest but this time with a raucous yikker. He then lands on a nearby post or rock with his prey until the female crashes into him and takes over the food. This is all done at very high speed and with a great deal of noise. A kind of punk-rock food pass as opposed to the harrier's string quartet.

At this time of year, the moors are alive with large insects such as northern eggar moths that dash over the heather, and small birds such as meadow pipits, skylarks and whinchats. These form the bulk of the merlin's diet, whereas hen harriers are also rather fond of mice, voles, lizards and the occasional red grouse, a habit which has brought it into conflict with man. As the sun began to set, we watched a pair of curlew calling above their nest site and we flushed a male black grouse from a damp area where it had probably been feeding on the nutritious heads of cotton grass. It's no wonder that the moors are my favourite habitat.

June 23rd It's not often that I visit Caernarfon these days but when I do, it brings back fond memories of my childhood when I would walk around the town with my Taid. At that time, it was a lively and energetic place but now, despite its local characters, it has become old, wrinkled and run-down. The castle is still its most important tourist attraction and a day's filming within the grounds showed that it's also a great attraction for wildlife.

Rock pipits are birds that I generally associate with rocky coasts and I suppose a castle overlooking the Menai Straits fits the bill from a pipit's point of view. At least three males were doing their 'parachute' display by gaining height and floating down on open wings and raised tails. The cracked masonry provides plenty of nesting sites and on a hot summer's day, insects were buzzing around by the thousand.

The walls themselves are home to plenty of plants including red valerian, a rather beautiful garden escapee. I also saw maidenhair spleenwort, wall pennywort and dozens of lichens that I couldn't begin to identify. Feral pigeons used some of the deeper holes as nesting sites and herring gulls were a constant threat to anyone eating sandwiches or chips. These are now seen as pests in most of our coastal towns and cities and although I'm no fan of raucous gulls, I'm a great admirer of their ability to thrive alongside man.

June 24th After weeks of fine, dry weather, the heavens opened with a vengeance today with a symphony of thunder and lightning starting the proceedings at four o'clock in the morning. Despite this, a respite mid-morning allowed me to go for a run along the canal with the dogs and to check on the common sandpiper's nest near Aber- miwl bridge. At the beginning of the week, one egg had been kicked out by the sitting bird, presumably when she was disturbed off the nest. I replaced it, not knowing how long it had been left unattended, and when I visited the site this morning, I found that three of the eggs had hatched. The adults had moved onto a more extensive area of shingle nearby with the youngsters, leaving a single egg in the nest scrape. I can only presume that the egg I found had become cold and infertile, but at least three of the chicks hatched successfully.

My mum telephoned this morning to tell me that she and my father had heard a corncrake calling from a hay meadow on Ynys Enlli (Bardsey) at the beginning of the week. They used to nest on the island until just after the Second World War and they disappeared from Wales completely as a regular breeding species during the 1970s. With the population in Scotland now recovering, there is some hope that they may return to Wales to nest in the near future but it will take a major agricultural revolution before they can do so.

Mum also told me that an old friend of hers had been overjoyed at the sight of a red kite flying over the village of Caeathro, near Caernarfon. She grew up in the village and it must be a dream come true for her to see this magnificent bird back in the area for the first time in well over a century. Two years ago, I took my father back to his native area near Cwmllynfell in the upper Swansea valley and he had tears in his eyes when we watched a kite circle over Fforch Egel farm where he used to live. The kite is more than just a bird to the people of Wales, it is a symbol of hope and success for a nation that has been downtrodden over the centuries.

Talking of downtrodden Welshmen, Clive Woodward has chosen eight Englishmen and only four Welshmen for the first Lions test against the All Blacks tomorrow. The last four tour games have seen four Welshmen give man-of-the-match performances. Only two make the test team. Enough said.

June 26th With my wife away on a course over the weekend, the boys and I have had a great time looking for all kinds of wildlife. Yesterday, we went down to a lovely meadow along the banks of the Severn to find that hundreds of meadow brown butterflies had appeared almost overnight. Their slow, unpredictable flight and the fact that they never appeared to land in the strong sunlight made them difficult to photograph, unlike the beautiful, orange-winged common skippers that darted from flower to flower and took great delight in relieving the hawkweeds of their nectar.

Last night, the tawny owls from the woodland opposite the house decided to bring their offspring into our garden around midnight, waking both the dogs and Tomos, our youngest son. He asked me whether there were monsters on the roof and I explained that they were young owls. We both went outside to see and one of the juveniles sat on the chimney for several minutes before flying off into the darkness. Tomos slept contentedly after that, safe in the knowledge that any monster foolish enough to visit the garden would be attacked by 'his' owl.

On the way home from Ynys-las this afternoon, I scared the living daylights out of a tabby cat and made it drop the young rabbit it was

SLOW-WORM (photo: Steve Phillipps)

carrying in its mouth. I pulled over and was pleased to find that the rabbit was shocked but unharmed, so I released it into some dense undergrowth nearby. I'm not a fan of domestic cats, especially as they kill so many wild animals throughout Britain including, it is said, significant numbers of reptiles such as slow-worms and common lizards. With two dogs in the house, not many cats venture into our garden but next door's large tabby knows when the dogs are locked in and walks past the window to send them wild. It has to be said, he's one cool cat.

June 27th I was awake very early this morning and shortly after dawn, I was sat outside on the bench listening to a curlew calling from some fields below the village. These fields are generally cut for silage but this year, the new owner will cut hay in early July and a few weeks ago, I noticed a curlew walking amongst a sea of buttercups and sorrel. They now have chicks, according to the local postman, and another few days should see them fledge successfully.

Once Ceri had taken the boys to school, I took the dogs for a run along the canal and because of the bright sunlight, the place was alive with damselflies and dragonflies. A pair of moorhen has nested where a hawthorn branch, swamped with reed canary grass, has extended out into the canal. The nest is very difficult to see but today, the adults were swimming across open water with their brood. Last year, both pairs that nest between Aber-miwl and Aberbechan failed, probably because of mink, and this pair still have a few weeks to go before the youngsters fledge. With all the vegetation along the banks, it will be difficult to keep up with their progress, but hopefully it will also mean that they are hidden from predators.

It's been a very good year for bullfinches here in mid Wales and as I finished my run this morning, I came across four chicks that were just about to leave their nest in a dense dog rose bush. They were fully feathered but all still had the straggly down feathers around the eyebrows that gave them that Dennis Healey look. At this stage, they are very vulnerable to predators such as cats and sparrowhawks so I left them well alone and carried on with my running.

June 28th Today, we started filming on the second of the BBC's programmes on Welsh canals and this time, it was the turn of the Montgomeryshire Canal. This is the one that ran from Shropshire, up the Severn valley, as far as Newtown and although the last couple of miles are now dry, the rest of it is still there and has become a haven for wildlife. So much so that it has now been designated a Site of Special Scientific Interest.

A small section of the canal, between Welsh Frankton and Maesbury, is now open to boats but because it's not heavily used, it's still a great place for wildlife. All along the banks, I saw a variety of wild flowers including two well-established introductions, monkeyflower and ivy-leaved toadflax. The yellow monkeyflower was introduced from Alaskan islands in the early nineteenth century, but it has become well-established in damp areas throughout Britain. The ivy-leaved toadflax is a creeper that grows on walls and banks and although it originates in southern Europe, it has settled rather well here in Britain. Behind one clump of toadflax on a lock wall, a female pied wagtail stared back at me from her nest.

Newly-emerged brown hawker dragonflies patrolled certain sections of the canal, defending their territories against all comers. They have yellow-brown wings that glisten in the sun and are absent from Wales apart from some canals and ponds along the English border. Like all dragonflies, they have excellent vision and fly rapidly over waterside vegetation in search of their insect prey. We also encountered clouds of horseflies where the canal bisected some wet meadows and alder woodlands. It's a shame the brown hawkers couldn't eat more of these nasty beasties.

June 29th We moved along the Montgomeryshire Canal with its wealth of large-leaved water dock and purple-flowered woundwort until we reached the beautiful village of Aberriw. Here, the canal crosses the river Rhiw with its cascading waterfalls frequented by a family of grey wagtails. As we ate our lunch, I watched the parents fly repeatedly into a pipe entrance in a brick wall where a nest full of hungry chicks awaited them. They feed on insects such as mayflies and stoneflies around the water's edge, their tails constantly wagging to an inaudible beat.

ELVIS AND THE HOBBIES

'This morning, I visited Cardiff Bay for the first time in many years. I first went there in the early 1980s when it was a wildlife-rich estuary where thousands of dunlin, redshank, curlew and shelduck gathered each autumn and winter.'

GIANT HOGWEED

July 1st It always amazes me how woodland birds fall silent on or around July 1st. This morning, I heard a few song thrushes and chiffchaffs but many of the birds that had been warbling to great effect in April, May and June seem to have lost their voices. They are still around but their priorities have changed. Attracting a mate or keeping neighbours at bay are no longer issues; their mission now is to skulk around out of the reach of predators and feed the family.

Over the past few days, thousands of tiny frogs have been emerging from the still waters. They have gone through the miraculous process of metamorphosis where they changed from tadpoles into froglets and now they must escape the water in search of cool, damp places in the surrounding fields and hedgerows. I've watched herons gorge themselves on hundreds of these small frogs but the strategy of all emerging at once ensures that some will eventually return to the canal to breed. The speed of their development depends on a variety of different factors including the temperature of the water – spawn develops faster in warmer water – and the availability of food. It has been said that tadpoles in nutrient-poor upland ponds can take over a year to develop into small frogs but the Montgomeryshire Canal is ideal for them.

The hedgerows along the edge of the canal are decorated by a plant with beautiful, purple flowers called hedge woundwort. It gets its name

COMMON FROG (photo: Steve Phillipps)

because in olden times, the leaves were crushed into a poultice and used to disinfect open wounds. The flowers are quite stunning, their gaping mouths resembling small snapdragons.

July 2nd Although the giant hogweed is an invasive, introduced species, its enormous flowers are quite spectacular. Beneath Aber-miwl bridge, over a dozen plants stand tall over all the other grasses and brambles, their white compound flowers like enormous satellite dishes. Dewi, my son, was dwarfed by one of them when he stood next to it this afternoon and although I'm over six feet tall, the hogweeds towered over my head too. By the end of the summer, several hundreds of their seeds will have fallen into the river Severn to colonize new areas along its bank. Eventually, no river bank will be free of this poisonous alien.

July 3rd This afternoon, I visited the small mixed woodland where, earlier in the spring, I had located a pair of goshawks. By now, had the pair nested successfully, the young would have fledged and therefore I was able to walk along the footpath that bisected the wood safe in the knowledge that I would not be causing any unnecessary disturbance.

As I approached the stand of dense Douglas fir where I had previously seen the birds, I came across the remains of several crows. Most had been recently-fledged youngsters, inexperienced and unsure on the wing, therefore easy prey for a hungry bird of prey. The nest itself was situated in a tall birch surrounded by conifers, the white down feathers on the edge of the nest a sure sign that it had been used this spring. I walked on along the path, not wanting to dawdle too near the nest, when I flushed a juvenile goshawk from a fresh pigeon carcass. The prey had been beheaded and plucked clean by the adult before being passed on to the juvenile who was in the process of feasting on the large flight muscles and some of the vital organs.

As I left the woodland, I heard three jays keeping the devil of a noise in a stand of Sitka spruce. Closer inspection showed that they were mobbing a large adult female goshawk, two drawing the hawk's attention whilst the third pecked at its tail. The words 'playing with fire' come to mind.

July 4th Whilst walking through the back field with the dogs today, we found a newly fledged buzzard in amongst the uncut hay. It was malnourished and soaking wet with no sign of its parents, so I retrieved a dead rabbit from the road outside the village and fed parts of the hind legs to the bird. Once I had dried it a little with an old towel, I placed it out of harm's way in a hawthorn beneath its nest in a tall oak tree.

It was a beautiful bird with grey eyes and reddish tinge all over its wing coverts and tail. Unlike young sparrowhawks and kestrels, juvenile buzzards are generally fairly docile but it pays to be wary of their bright yellow talons. They have fairly short, strong toes that are ideal for walking across fields in search of earthworms and beetles but they are just as well-adapted for grasping young rabbits and voles before the strong beak gives the *coup de grâce*. It was a real pleasure being so close to such a wild bird, albeit under rather unfortunate circumstances.

July 6th Yesterday was a thoroughly miserable, wet day filming on the Brecon and Monmouth Canal. Today was much calmer and drier and it was wonderful to be able to travel along the waterway at four miles per hour watching the world go by.

In the afternoon, we left the canal and travelled up the Blorenge mountain, overlooking Abergavenny, to the Punchbowl. This is a Woodland Trust reserve containing ancient beech trees, some over 300 years old, unimproved grassland and a large pond full of dragonflies, newts and frogs. It is surrounded by moorland full of whinchats and meadow pipits, and the unimproved pastures are alive with anthills which, in turn, attract green woodpeckers. It is a magical site in the heart of a wild upland area on the edge of the industrial south Wales valleys.

July 7th The area around Abergavenny is the stronghold for the hobby in Wales. This is an agile, long-winged falcon that superficially resembles the peregrine but is more streamlined. Indeed, it is such a supreme flier that it is able to catch dragonflies, swallows and even swifts in flight. It first nested in Wales in the 1960s but soon spread along the eastern counties and today it is a widespread, but still rather sparse, breeding bird.

This morning, I watched one chase after sand martins above the river Usk. Despite several attempts, it was unsuccessful in its hunting and it gradually gave up and concentrated instead on chasing dragonflies above the canal. Here, it was more successful and within a few minutes, it had caught two large emperor dragonflies. These, it ate on the wing whilst circling above our boat before returning to hunt once more. Eventually, we lost sight of it behind some alder trees but it had been a magical few minutes in the company of one of our most elusive birds of prey.

July 8th I hadn't seen mink on any of the Welsh canals for quite some time and there is talk that they are gradually being ousted by the returning otter. This morning, however, I watched one of these American impostors searching the banks of the Monmouthshire and Brecon Canal in search of food. This might explain why, in three hours of travelling, we saw only one pair of moorhen. Several locals told me that in the past, moorhens were commonly seen on every section of the waterway but since colonization by mink, they are now confined principally to the more urban areas. It's a familiar tale throughout Wales.

I had a particularly interesting conversation with a man from Gofilon who described how he lost 27 ornamental fish from his pond in one night. The following morning, whilst eating breakfast in his conservatory, he watched an otter dive into the pond to retrieve the last of the remaining fish. Once he'd finished his meal, the otter casually rubbed his head against the conservatory before making his way across the garden to the canal. If you're going to lose your ornamental fish to a wild creature, better an otter than a mink.

Like all of our canals, the Mon and Brec (as the locals call it) is full of fish. We watched several pike, perch and roach hiding amongst the aquatic vegetation and in one particularly wide section of water, we came across a group of enormous carp. There were at least half a dozen of them and not one of them was under 15 pounds in weight. They would swim around in the shallows, stirring up the mud, and feed on the many invertebrates that were carried up to the surface. Interestingly, the only fishermen we saw were in the areas of least fish but the herons congregated in the areas where fish were plentiful.

July 9th I'm constantly amazed by the way in which our roadside verges, if left uncut, change colour from one month to the next. A few weeks ago, they were dominated by cow parsley and red campion but now, they have largely gone to seed to be replaced by a variety of other flowers. Even the ox-eye daisies that dominated the banks until recently, have been swamped by the tall grasses and leaves of the recent 'arrivals'. One of these is a member of the umbellifers, or the family that includes the cow parsley and pig nut, called the upright hedge parsley. Superficially, it resembles cow parsley but the compound flowers are smaller with a pinkish hue and the leaves are pinnate. It was particularly common on the hill road between Llanbadarn and Dolfor, on the way to Llandrindod, where its small pink heads could be seen peeping above the taller grasses.

Moorhens have had little success on the Montgomeryshire canal in recent years but today, I saw an adult with seven well grown youngsters. When I approached, the female didn't alarm-call but merely flicked her tail, exposing the white flashes, and the chicks all ran for cover along the wide water lily leaves. A short distance further along, another pair has built a nest from horsetails in the middle of a particularly deep pool. Whether they survive in such an open area is doubtful and I don't imagine it will be long before the local mink come calling.

July 10th Today, I walked along the canal for the first time in quite a while. Usually, I run along its banks several times every week but the late morning walk in bright sunshine paid dividends immediately when I heard a rustling noise in the dead leaves along the edge of the canal. It was not the loud rustling of a blackbird in search of earthworms nor the heavy-footed rustling of a rabbit scurrying into the undergrowth. It was a smooth and constant rustling and further investigation revealed a small grass snake searching for prey.

At first, I could only make out its dark olive tail but patience was rewarded when its head, complete with bright yellow collar, popped up from between the leaves. Its tongue darted out to taste the air and then it continued on its way. It was not a particularly large individual, probably no more than 30 centimetres in length, but it's the first time I've seen one along the canal for four years. I shall have to do more walking and less running if I want to see the wildlife in future.

July 12th I love Welsh rivers. Each one has its own distinctive character and this morning, I walked the dogs along the middle section of the river Wye below Builth. The path we followed was bordered by an amazing variety of plants including the delightfully named enchanters' nightshade with its small, delicate white flowers. Its leaves are similar to those of dog's mercury and as both love the more shady areas, it can be quite confusing. Another plant that was flowering along the verge was crosswort but this loves the more sunny areas and its small yellow flowers look like specks of glitter. Probably the most obvious and tallest of the flowers were the deep pink spikes of rosebay willowherb, a plant that is called fireweed in North America because it immediately colonizes burnt areas and cleared ground. As a child, I remember finding the huge, finger-sized caterpillars of elephant hawkmoths feeding on the leaves but despite a thorough search, I found nothing this morning.

wild about the wild | elvis and the hobbies

In the late afternoon, we filmed on some semi-natural grasslands on reclaimed coal slag overlooking the village of Quakers' Yard. It was full of bird's-foot trefoil and knapweed as well as over a dozen different types of grasses, and meadow brown butterflies were fluttering to and fro with the gusts of wind. It's wonderful to be able to note that many farmers have delayed cutting their grass until early July this year, long enough for many of the plants to seed and for curlews to rear their chicks, and I'm pleased that those farmers are having a wonderfully sunny week for their harvest.

July 13th This afternoon, it was nice to be able to visit a place I'd never set foot on previously, an area of land overlooking the river Taf known as Pontypridd Common. This is a public park which is also common land and unlike most parks I know, large sections of it have been allowed to grow wild. This means that heather, rosebay willowherb and bracken dominate rather than rye grass and exotic flowers. Some beautiful native flowers such as sheep's bit and harebells were also beginning to show their blue heads in some places.

HAREBELLS AND KNAPWEED

The common is said to support adders and although many areas looked suitable, I failed to find any evidence of their presence. I did, however, manage to find several common lizards sunbathing on the rocky outcrops and paths and the tall grasses were full of vole and mouse holes. With all this prey around, I'm sure there are adders in there somewhere and I hope that the locals appreciate them enough to leave them in peace. The young lads I met were more interested in rugby and women than adders but I, for one, wouldn't judge them for that!

July 14th Last night I stayed in Cardiff so that we could have an early start at Forest Farm, a peaceful wildlife haven on the northern outskirts of the city. It is located on the route of the old Glamorganshire Canal and the few remaining wet areas now support good numbers of dragonflies and damselflies. Most are common enough but the hairy dragonfly is very scarce in Wales. It has, as its name suggests, a very hairy thorax and although I was too late to see them fly, the warden showed me one he'd picked up dead a few days earlier.

It was a joy to watch some territorial demoiselles, both the banded and beautiful demoiselle, dancing in the few sunlit areas along the canal, keeping neighbours away from their favoured areas. Whereas the banded has a blue-green band on its wing, the beautiful is an iridescent green all over, but both are striking insects, especially when seen in bright sunlight.

HONEY BUZZARD AND CHICKS (photo: Steve Phillipps)

July 15th This morning, I visited Cardiff Bay for the first time in many years. I first went there in the early 1980s when it was a wildlife-rich estuary where thousands of dunlin, redshank, curlew and shelduck gathered each autumn and winter. During the 1990s, in one of the most blatant acts of mindless environmental vandalism by any British government, the estuary was blocked off by a huge barrage to form what is now known as Cardiff Bay. Needless to say, the thousands of wading birds and wildfowl have disappeared and it was ironic to find statues of brass curlews looking out over the bay.

On the way back up to mid Wales, I made a detour so that I could visit the Afan Argoed Forest Visitors' Centre near Pont-rhyd-y-fen, a few miles north of Port Talbot. The centre is best known for its mountain biking but it also has a coalmining museum and today, another new attraction was opened. The RSPB and Forest Enterprise have cooperated with Wales Raptor Study Group workers to put a video camera on a honey buzzard nest, the first time this has been done in the UK. This afternoon, with much pomp and ceremony, they officially launched the live link.

Honey buzzards are fascinating birds because, unlike most other birds of prey, they don't swoop down from the skies to tear a rabbit or vole to pieces, rather they dig out wasp nests to devour the grubs. They are well adapted to do this because their toes are short and strong for digging and the feathers around the head are extremely dense so that the wasps are unable to get at their sensitive skin.

For years, so-called experts were telling us that honey buzzards couldn't survive the wet, cold weather of upland Wales, the north of England and Scotland but today in these areas, honey buzzards are widely distributed. In Wales, the first pair was found in 1991 and since then, several nests are found each year in upland conifer plantations. One of the principal reasons why several pairs go undetected is because, at a glance, they are so similar to the widespread common buzzard.

The nest featured at Afan Argoed is high up in a conifer tree and contains one young chick. Typical of this species, there is a great deal of greenery around the nest cup and scattered all over the nest platform are remnants of wasp comb that used to contain the grubs that form the birds' staple diet. It is hoped that all this video footage can be analysed so that we can learn even more about this rare and mysterious bird.

July 16th On the radio this morning, I learned that bearded tits have nested in Wales for the first time in over 20 years. These are small, reed-bed-dwelling birds with rusty-brown bodies, long tails and a striking dark moustache. They are fairly common in the fens of East Anglia and now that the pair at the Gwent Levels have reared six young, it is hoped that they will colonize other wetland areas in Wales. The avocets have also had a successful nesting season on the levels with three out of four pairs breeding successfully.

July 17th I am an inveterate log turner. I cannot walk past a log or piece of corrugated iron without carefully turning it over to explore its dark side. This afternoon, my obsessive log-turning paid handsome dividends as not only did the boys and myself find a bank vole staring up at us, we also found a nest containing at least seven young. I regularly find old, empty nests but this was the first active nest I'd found all year and after taking a quick photograph of the blind youngsters, only a few days old, I replaced the oak log.

Bank voles, along with field voles and wood mice, are fair game for all comers in the open countryside. Whether you're a kestrel, stoat, polecat, buzzard, grass snake or domestic cat, mice and voles feature prominently on your menu. Because of this, they produce several large litters every year and in times of plenty, they will breed almost all year round. Soon, instead of one or two mice and voles in your hay field, you will have thousands and if it weren't for the predators, our fields would be overrun with them.

BANK VOLE NEST WITH YOUNG

July 18th Three years ago, I opened Butterfly Conservation's first reserve in Wales, Euarth Rocks near Rhuthun. It's an area of limestone pavement that has become overgrown with scrub and bracken in recent years but it holds 32 species of butterfly. Since I last visited the site, a group of volunteers has been bashing the scrub in order to encourage plants such as violets and bird's-foot trefoil that will, in turn, encourage

scarce butterflies such as the pearl-bordered fritillary. So far, the signs are encouraging but, unfortunately, when I walked around the reserve this morning, the constant drizzle meant that all we saw were a few meadow browns.

I drove back home over the Berwyn moors in the hope of catching a glimpse of a late hen harrier or short-eared owl but high summer is not a good time to look for birds on these uplands. However, the gorse is beginning to come into bloom and the stone wall leading off the moor towards the village of Llangynog is lined with a delicate-looking plant called the parsley fern. It is so-called because the leaves look like parsley and in Welsh, one of its names, *rhedynen y chwarel*, means 'quarry fern' because it is often found growing in the rubble of old quarry and mine workings, especially the slate quarries of north Wales.

Back home, the saddest event of the day was finding the buzzard chick that I had attempted to rescue at the beginning of the month. Then, it

PARSLEY FERN

had been emaciated but this afternoon, it was long dead. It's a sad tale but it's a fate that befalls more than 50% of our breeding birds within the first few weeks of leaving the nest. Besides, I can take some small comfort from the fact that the buzzard is our most widespread bird of prey and this part of the Welsh Marches is one of its strongholds.

July 20th Hazelnuts have been poking their white noses out from between the round, green hazel leaves for the past couple of weeks and is it my imagination, or are they appearing earlier than they used to? They won't be ready to eat for another month or more but I'm sure that when I was growing up, we would never find a fully mature nut before the middle of September. This is where keeping detailed records over a long period of time is so useful but in those days, watching wildlife had to compete with chasing girls and rugby balls. These days, I can't catch either of the latter two so there's plenty of time for the wildlife.

July 21st A busy day for the boys and myself because we left home early to visit Steve Roberts and his family near Abergavenny. Steve is Tomos's godfather and the boys love visiting his house because he's a kind of Welsh 'Crocodile Dundee'.

We spent the day swimming in the river Usk whilst a kingfisher and several grey wagtails sped past, and walking the fields around the hamlet of Llanfair Cilgedin. It's a beautiful part of Wales and the final stronghold of the turtle dove, a bird that was once widespread throughout the lowlands. Although we didn't see any of these

DEWI AND AUSTRALIAN CARPET PYTHON

wild about the wild | elvis and the hobbies

rare birds, woodpigeons were abundant, feeding on the corn spilled by the combine harvesters and tractors as they went about their business in the surrounding cereal fields.

Unfortunately, we weren't able to stay until the evening when Steve was meeting up with some colleagues to ring a brood of hobbies. The boys would have loved to have seen their Uncle Steve doing his Tarzan bit but back home, a friend from the University of Cardiff was calling by with a few snakes. Rhys Jones is one of Wales's foremost herpetologists and I'd met him whilst filming a BBC series in the spring. He'd come to visit so that we could go out with a local naturalist to see some badgers but as he keeps some exotic snakes, he said he'd bring some up with him.

We weren't disappointed because he'd brought six snakes in all, three of which were over two metres in length. Despite their size, the golden python, Australian carpet python and red-tailed boa constrictors were completely bomb proof and my two boys warmed to them immediately. The boys and the snakes had a wonderful evening exploring our garden but, from time to time, Rhys had to ensure that they didn't wander too far. By the end of the evening, several neighbours and friends had called by to see these wonderful animals and it was heart-warming to watch them handle these huge snakes despite their preconceived fears and phobias.

The three smaller snakes Rhys had brought with him were a little trickier to handle, especially the bull snake, a Canadian species that is not venomous but has a nasty bite nonetheless. Despite this, the evening went extremely well and my boys are now pestering me to take them down to Cardiff so that they can meet, as they so eloquently put it, some of Rhys's nasty snakes!

Before dark, we still had time to go once more with Gareth Morgan, a local character, to a local badger sett. These are no ordinary badgers, however, as Gareth has been visiting the same sett and feeding the badgers for over 20 years and by now, he literally has them feeding out of his hand. Several individuals, young and old, came up to him to beg for peanuts and digestive biscuits and I had to remind myself several times that these were truly wild animals. I had been to several so-called badger watches over the years, but none can compare with an evening in the company of Gareth and his family of badgers. A truly memorable day capped by an unforgettable evening.

July 23rd Following my early morning radio appearance today, I took the dogs to a mixed woodland near the town of Llanidloes. The larches were full of crossbills, a species that I had seen plenty of in late winter and early spring but since then, I hadn't come across a single bird. There were several flocks of about a dozen birds, all feeding on the cones ripening in the uppermost branches of the larches. Their 'jip-jip' calls filled the woodland and I had stunning views of both males and females in the early morning light. I even found some crossbill feathers along one of the paths – probably a recent sparrowhawk victim.

It's always a sure sign that the breeding season is drawing to a close when you find mixed tit flocks wandering through your local woods. This evening, I walked the dogs around the village and watched a flock of about ten great, blue and coal tits feeding amongst the leaves of a tall hawthorn hedge. They never stay still for long, constantly moving from branch to branch and leaf to leaf in search of caterpillars and other insects.

July 24th Just over a week ago, I went down to Afan Argoed near Port Talbot to see a video link to a honey buzzards' nest being officially opened. At that time, there was one healthy chick in the nest. A few days ago, some of the forestry rangers watched wide-eyed as a goshawk landed on the nest and proceeded to kill and eat the chick. It must have been awful to watch this scenario unfold knowing that there wasn't anything they could do about it because the nest was so far away.

July 26th I began filming the last programme in the series on Welsh canals today and we spent most of the morning in the Neath valley. Much of the derelict urban areas around Neath itself have become overgrown with buddleia, an introduced shrub that was imported into parks and gardens. Generally, the purple flowers attract hundreds of butterflies such as peacock, red admiral and small tortoiseshell but today, I didn't see a single one. It has been an awful year for butterflies in general but the three species I mention above have had a dreadful summer. Thankfully, I don't think it's a sudden decline, rather a seasonal dip that occurs every so often.

Later in the morning, we walked along the Tennent Canal towpath as it skirts around Pant-y-Sais fen in the company of the Countryside Council of Wales warden and wildlife enthusiast, David Painter. He is an excellent naturalist, pointing out some of the riparian plants such as the beautiful yellow flowers of yellow loosestrife and greater spearwort. But we had actually come in search of Britain's biggest spider.

The raft spider was previously known from only two sites in south-east England until, three years ago, a small population was found along the banks of the Tennent Canal. At most times of the year, they are virtually impossible to see because they hibernate beneath dense vegetation in winter but in high summer, the females build a webbed dome to house their 150 or so spiderlings. She then stands guard nearby to ward off any marauding insects until the young disperse.

We were very fortunate in finding five females, four with a nest of spiderlings and one carrying an egg sack beneath its body. They are chocolate brown in colour with two yellow stripes along the thorax and, as David so aptly described them, they are about the size of a 50 pence piece with long legs. It's incredible to think that the colony, which numbers around 50 females, is confined to one 800-metre section of canal. If anything happens to that part of the canal, the spiders become extinct.

July 27th Back down south to film canals, but this time, the Swansea Canal between Ynysmeudwy and Clydach. Here, the banks are overgrown with alien species such as Himalayan balsam and Japanese knotweed but there are some pockets of beautiful native species such as yellow and purple loosestrife, the latter just beginning to come into flower.

Whilst filming along a section that was smothered in knotweed, I watched a family of moorhens feeding along the far bank and I was fascinated to see that the adult birds had two generations of youngsters. Generally in the bird world, the youngsters are kicked out by the adults once they are independent but with moorhens, individuals from earlier broods will help the adults rear the next batch of juveniles. This works both ways because the adults are given assistance to rear their young whereas the older juveniles gain valuable experience for when they rear their own young in future years.

July 28th Another journey to the Neath valley, but an interesting stop en route near the old railway station at Erwood. I stop on long journeys to walk the dogs and Erwood is one of my favoured areas because it's halfway and it has lovely walks both along the Wye and on the hills. This morning, I listened to three male yellowhammers calling together as I walked through shoulder-high bracken, their beautiful yellow plumage resplendent in the meagre sunlight. Because they are late nesters, the males will sing until the end of the month but it's not often one hears three singing together in Wales these days.

The *ffridd* around Erwood is also a great area for breeding stonechats and some of the late broods scattered into the surrounding gorse bushes as the dogs forged ahead. I also listened to two chiffchaffs calling from the hawthorn bushes, birds I hadn't heard, let alone seen, for several weeks. Breeding chiffchaffs generally become quiet around the first week of July but after a brief respite, some birds begin to call again towards the end of the month. Whether these are recent immigrants or local breeders, I don't know, but it's heartening to hear some song, albeit a monotonous chiffchaff, so late in the summer.

Lorocal authorities all over Wales are frantically trying to uproot thousands of ragwort plants before the yellow flowers turn to seed. It's a shame that it's so universally disliked because it's wonderful for wildlife and this afternoon, I found several plants whose leaves were being devoured by the orange and black caterpillars of the cinnabar moth. The adult moths are bright red and black, the striking colours on both adults and caterpillars indicating to any would-be predator that they are highly toxic. Without ragwort plants to feed on, the cinnabar moth will disappear.

July 30th The crossbill invasion I noted a week ago has continued with large numbers recorded throughout the Hafren Forest near Llanidloes this morning. Everywhere I went, I heard and saw flocks feeding on the pine cones, whether they were larch or Sitka spruce trees. Some of the birds were scaly juveniles, indicating a good breeding season. On the contrary, however, siskins have been scarce this spring and summer following several good breeding seasons, although why that should be so with such a good cone crop is a mystery to me.

The dogs disturbed a woodcock from a wide ride in the middle of a large larch plantation and although I saw no evidence of breeding, I called the dogs away regardless. As a youngster, I'd find woodcock nests most years but it has certainly become much scarcer in the conifer woodlands of mid Wales over the past 25 years. In winter, of course, numbers are augmented by the influx of thousands of birds from Russia and Scandinavia but they don't usually arrive this far west until late October.

Our resident female house spiders, Elvis and Aaron, have both produced spiderlings over the past two weeks and every morning, one of my tasks is to clear the bath of these recent invaders. I'm quite willing to tolerate several large spiders in the house but visitors may object to a house overrun by these eight-legged creatures. Elvis lives in our utility and Aaron in the toilet and between them, they rid the place of dozens of bluebottles, houseflies and midges each year. All I need now is to attract bats to the attic!

July 31st My brother and his three children have come up for the weekend and today, we walked along the Mochdre brook on the outskirts of Newtown where it runs along an unimproved field and into the Severn. At this time of year, the lobster-like signal crayfish are difficult to find because they shed their hard outer layer in order to grow. They therefore skulk under rocks and banks out of harm's way until the 'new' shell has hardened.

We did, however, manage to find two large individuals, both with soft shells, and it was a wonderful opportunity for the children to be able to hold a creature that usually they shy away from because of their evil-looking pincers. With soft pincers, they are unable to defend themselves and they become an easy target for any passing otter, mink or heron, as well as young children. Whilst searching under rocks, we found a variety of other creatures, including leeches, stone loaches and bullheads, caddis-fly larvae cases and a large toad.

The unimproved meadow is a terrific place for wildlife because it hasn't seen fertilizer for decades. In spring, it's full of primroses and cowslips and now, in late summer, lesser knapweed with their thistle-like flowers. It's also a wonderful place to learn to recognise your grasses but I'm afraid I start to get confused once I get beyond cocksfoot and a few others.

As we walked through the tall grasses, butterflies flew from flower to flower. Most were meadow browns, one of the few species of butterflies that will fly in dull weather. The meadow brown's caterpillar feeds on grasses, therefore this was an ideal site for them, but we also came across one red admiral and a few small coppers in an area dominated by dock and sorrel, its favoured food plants.

By the end of the day, the children were all soaking, having spent so much time in the stream, but they'd had a great time and, hopefully, learned something about Wales's wonderful wildlife.

ALASKA AND THE EISTEDDFOD

'Having had a whole day to explore the sights of Anchorage and recover from our transatlantic journey, we boarded a worryingly small plane for the journey to the tiny and remote village of Port Alsworth.'

COMMON BLUE BUTTERFLIES MATING (photo: Steve Phillipps)

August 1st This morning, I went undercover to film that most despicable of practices, the illegal trapping of birds of prey. We were in a woodland north of Dundee in Scotland and having passed several legal pheasant pens, we found pens surrounded by illegally-set fenn traps.

Fenn traps are spring traps that are used legally to catch stoats, weasels and rats but they are supposed to be set underground or hidden away in a stone wall where other creatures can't be caught. The traps we found this morning were set out in the open and baited with dead pheasants in order to attract foxes, badgers, pine marten, buzzards and goshawks. We quickly filmed the scene and then beat a hasty retreat before calling the local police as they have both the authority and the expertise to deal with such matters.

I am actually quite supportive of legal gamekeeping as it keeps a semblance of control on the numbers of predators such as carrion crows and magpies but I abhor animal cruelty, and they don't come much worse than spring traps that are used illegally. Any passing buzzard that lands on one of these traps will have its legs broken but it will hang listlessly until it is dispatched by the gamekeeper several hours later. In the meantime, it will lie in excruciating pain, unable to fly or stand. Anyone who can set such traps, in my book, deserves every misfortune he gets.

Apart from the unpleasantness of finding illegal traps, the visit to Scotland was a pleasurable one. Not only was I able to catch up with old friends, I was also able to watch red squirrels and roe deer scampering about the wood. Grey squirrels have yet to arrive in this part of Scotland and reds are still very common, as are pine marten, although we failed to see a single one. At one time, when we were skulking around the pheasant pens, a startled roe deer scared the living daylights out of me as I thought I'd stumbled across one of the gamekeepers. Usually, animals are more frightened of us than we are of them but in the case of that one roe deer, I'm not so sure.

August 2nd When I awoke at home this morning, I was immediately struck by the absence of screaming swifts. Like clockwork, they leave mid Wales on the first of August having not arrived until around the first of May. For the next few weeks, I may see the odd straggler but the vast majority have now left us for Africa and with them has gone one of the principal elements of summer. I hate to be melodramatic but, for me, once the swifts have gone and the hours of daylight visibly shorten, I always feel that winter is just around the corner.

August 3rd I called by the local garage today to pick up a few odds and ends for the car and to check up on the progress of the resident pair of swallows. Peter, the owner, is delighted that he keeps getting a pair of swallows nesting up on the metal beams above the garage entrance and so far this year, the pair have reared one brood of four and are about to fledge another brood of three. They do make a mess on the floor but, as Peter says, it's no inconvenience when you compare it to the thrill that he and his customers get from watching the young family develop. Who knows, they may rear one more brood yet but if they do, let's hope for a warm September.

I walked the dogs along the outskirts of town and on a piece of waste ground, I found a single wild pansy. It's a beautiful flower, much like a smaller and more delicate version of the garden pansy and, over the centuries, it has commonly been associated with love. In Shakespeare's *A Midsummer Night's Dream*, Oberon squeezes the juice of this pansy into Titania's eyes so that she falls in love with Bottom, but as in all such tales, the course of true love never runs smoothly.

August 4th Every year, I make the pilgrimage to that star attraction of Welsh culture, the National Eisteddfod. I'm no enthusiastic fan of singing, dancing and reciting, but I do enjoy going around the eisteddfod field to catch up with old friends and to buy the latest books. This year, the eisteddfod is in the grounds of the Faenol Estate on the outskirts of Bangor and on the banks of the Menai Straits, so I was hoping to see some wildlife in amongst the Welsh culture.

As it turned out, apart from the odd buzzard and a few herring gulls, wildlife was rather thin on the ground, but it was great to be able to visit

WILD PANSY

the various conservation stands to catch up on the latest news from the natural world. I learned that the Porthmadog ospreys have now succeeded in rearing two chicks, the second having undertaken its maiden flight just a few days ago. This is wonderful news for Wales because it's another natural attraction to add to the impressive list and already this year, more than 50,000 visitors have been to see these wonderful birds.

August 5th This morning, the two-acre field set aside for development on the outskirts of Aber-miwl was full of butterflies. I don't mean the odd butterfly here and there, but hundreds of them. By far the most common were the beautiful gatekeepers with their orange and dark brown wings with a single eye-spot in the top corners. Clouds of gatekeepers and meadow browns would rise from the purple flowers of thistles and knapweed before circling and alighting on another flower nearby. Interspersed amongst these were a few large whites and hundreds of small, cream-coloured moths that hid amongst the tall grasses.

The thistles supported several more species of insects, including both two-spot and seven-spot ladybirds that were feasting on the ample supply of aphids. Orange soldier beetles were also abundant on the flowers of ragwort and yarrow, mating pairs outnumbering single insects by about ten to one. Dewi, my seven-year-old son, couldn't believe the noise made by all the grasshoppers in the field and he was

GATEKEEPER BUTTERFLY

astounded when I explained that the noise was made by rubbing their hind legs against their abdomen. It's wonderful to be able to show my children the kinds of fields I took for granted as a boy and I hope that the housing boom comes to an abrupt end so that this wonderful site can be saved for wildlife.

August 6th Another beautiful day, so I ventured back down to the field near Aber-miwl, this time with my camera in tow. And I wasn't disappointed! Along with those butterflies that I saw yesterday, I spotted several small skippers, about half the size of your average butterfly with orange-brown upperwings and orange-buff underwings. At rest, they hold their wings at an angle but they fly at great speed from flower to flower.

In one hour, I saw more peacocks, red admirals and small tortoiseshells than I'd seen all summer and, on some bramble leaves, I saw my first painted lady of the year. This is a migratory species that arrives from the continent in varying numbers and although last year was an excellent one for this species, this summer has been very poor. They will sometimes attempt to breed, especially in the south-west of England, but they don't yet survive our harsh winters.

Perhaps the most aggressive butterfly of them all was a male common blue that fed mainly on the yellow flowers of bird's-foot trefoil. It simply would not tolerate another butterfly of any species anywhere near its favoured feeding areas and a passing intruder would be forced to indulge in a spiralling aerial dance before being escorted away. Truly a fantastic day for butterflies!

One edge of the field borders a hawthorn copse that is surrounded by dog rose and brambles and I was pleased to note so many robins' pincushions on the wild roses. Along the roadside hedges, they have been destroyed by council flails, but here they are thriving. One was enormous, about half the size of a tennis ball, the biggest I have ever seen.

The bright sunlight caught a flash of red in amongst the brambles and at first I thought it was a discarded Coke can. Closer inspection revealed that they were three berry-laden stalks of the lords-and-ladies, a plant that has undertaken a miraculous metamorphosis from its first appearance in early spring. At that time, it resembles a purple club enshrouded by a green hood only to die back in early summer and reappear at this time of year like a phoenix from the flames.

August 7th Just enough time to walk the dogs along the canal at first light this morning before setting out for Alaska with the family.

The shallow lagoons near the sewage farm were alive with mallard as this year's youngsters joined the adult flock. At this time of year, the males are in eclipse, which means that they are moulting their breeding season feathers. As a result of this, they are extremely drab and it's often difficult to distinguish between, for example, a male mallard and a male wigeon. They lose their major flight feathers all at once and therefore need to find safe havens where they can feed and roost with minimal risk of disturbance. Come autumn, however, they will have regained their Sunday best and from the end of the year onwards, mating will once again be on their minds.

Later in the morning, we began our journey to the far north-east of the United States, to a small village called Port Alsworth, some 150 kilometres from Anchorage, the Alaskan capital. Two years ago, I had filmed wolves, moose and grizzly bears in this area and now, I was hoping to take my family to see these wonderful animals.

LORDS-AND-LADIES

August 9th After a gruelling 28-hour journey with brief stops at Newark and Seattle, we arrived in Anchorage to a glorious sunny day and a wonderful view over Cook Inlet, named after Captain Cook, and the aptly-named Ship Creek. Alaska was, until 1876, a part of Russia but it was sold to America for the princely sum of $7.2 million. Had the Russians known about the forthcoming Cold War and the vast mineral wealth of the land, I'm sure they would have held on to it for another century or two.

Anchorage is not a large city, nor is it a particularly pretty one, but it does have character and the feel of a frontier town. Black-capped chickadees, very similar to our marsh tits, played and fed in many of the garden bushes around town but probably the commonest bird was the magpie, or the black-billed magpie, to give it its American name. Another familiar species, Canada geese, were confined principally to the salt-marsh along the eastern shores of the inlet although the odd brave individual did venture inland from time to time.

August 11th Having had a whole day to explore the sights of Anchorage and recover from our transatlantic journey, we boarded a worryingly small plane for the journey to the tiny and remote village of Port Alsworth. The flight took us through Lake Clark Pass that is, in good weather, one of the most spectacular sights on the face of this Earth with its craggy mountain tops, crumbling glaciers and meandering rivers. In poor weather, however, it is a death trap and over the years, many an unwary pilot has met his Maker along the sheer cliff faces.

Port Alsworth is a pleasant village situated along the shores of Lake Clark and Glen Alsworth, the grandson of the village's first inhabitant, was to be our guide for the next few days. As we walked from the plane to our log cabin, a pair of ravens kronked overhead, not with the deep, throaty *cronc* of Welsh ravens but with a more high-pitched Alaskan kronk!

I had time for a leisurely walk through the surrounding woodlands whose floors were dotted with fungi, amongst them the toxic fly agaric with its red cap and white spots, and ceps, or penny buns. The latter are common in some of the woodlands around mid Wales and are wonderfully tasty when cooked in butter with onions and garlic.

In the evening, we sat outside the cabin to admire the breathtaking scenery of Tanalian Mountain reflected in the calm waters of Lake Clark only to have to retreat to our beds once the mosquitoes discovered that some fresh Welsh blood had moved into the neighbourhood.

August 12th In the morning, Glen took us by float-plane to an area where the remote tundra was bisected by salmon-rich rivers. In July and August, hundreds of millions of bright red sockeye salmon make their way up their natal rivers to spawn having spent 2-4 years feeding in the Pacific Ocean. Once they have spawned, they die, but inevitably such a glut of food in a barren region attracts dozens of predators.

King amongst these is the grizzly bear and from the air, we saw more than 20 adults and cubs feeding on dead and dying salmon. We landed on a nearby lake and walked the few hundred metres to one of the many areas of snow that had escaped the heat of the midday sun. When the weather is uncomfortably hot, the bears will often sit on these snowy areas until the heat is more bearable and sure enough, we came across a mother and two young cubs. We approached carefully, never breaking the horizon, and talking constantly. We were told that you should never sneak up on a grizzly because then, you really are asking for trouble.

The mother knew we were there but because we kept our distance, she ignored us and continued to roll around in the snow with the cubs. Gradually, she moved away to a distance of about 150 metres then suddenly, for no apparent reason, she charged towards us at an alarming speed. Having 900 pounds of muscle, fir and teeth charging towards you is a rather unnerving experience but Glen calmly told us to stand up and talk loudly and amazingly, it worked. She stopped in her

GRIZZLY BEAR AND CUBS

Dewi and Tomos, with a Stuffed Wolf for Company!

tracks, sniffed the air, and walked calmly back to her cubs. It pays to have an experienced guide by your side when you go bear watching.

Eventually, she moved her cubs away to a small river full of salmon and we watched her fishing for over an hour. At first, she and the cubs fed on the meat but eventually, they ignored the flesh and merely fed on the eggs. In time, even this delicacy became monotonous and I watched in amazement as this huge carnivore ambled out of the water and began feeding on blueberries, delicately picking them with its massive claws. There must be some instinct that tells them to take in an ample supply of vitamin C, either that or the berries were just a welcome relief from fish.

Over the course of the afternoon, several bears came and went as we watched, mesmerized, from the top of a small bluff. I had very little time to enjoy the other wildlife that flourished around me but I did notice some dwarf fireweed growing in a small, fertile hollow and a beautiful purple flower with the wonderful name of monkshood. It was the bears, however, that took centre stage and it will be a day that will stay in my family's memories forever.

August 13th Despite being tempted many times, I've never been on an outward-bound holiday but today, I was going to put that right by rafting down the Tazemna river. The Tazemna is not blessed with miles of white water and huge waterfalls, but it does have its moments, especially where trees have partially blocked the flow and by the end of the day, we all knew we'd been in a battle.

It was another glorious summer's day with not a cloud in the sky and it was a good omen when, within five minutes of starting out, we saw a wolf by the water's edge. Wolves are one of my favourite animals because they are so well-adapted for life in these wildernesses. Their long legs carry them effortlessly over countless miles and they hunt in packs so that they can bring down animals much larger than themselves.

This individual, however, merely stared at us for a few seconds, then turned on his heels and loped back into the forest. As we passed the spot where he'd been standing, we searched in vain for any sign of him in the bushes but like a ghost, he'd disappeared. I'm sure there were other members of the pack nearby but they remained hidden, probably because in this part of North America, they are hunted for their fur and man is therefore the wolf's deadliest enemy.

Onwards we paddled, under the occasional fallen tree, with wolf and moose tracks scattered all along the river banks. We disturbed a red-breasted merganser with her brood of four chicks and a group of bufflehead, a duck that rather resembles a goldeneye but with a large white dot behind the eye. As we approached a slower-moving section of the river, we were extremely fortunate to see a beaver swimming from one bank to the other but when I tried to get close enough to take a photograph, it dived underwater and disappeared.

Closer inspection along the banks showed that it had been going ashore to cut down willow trees and dragging the branches back to the water to feed on the bark. We couldn't find a dam or lodge nearby but from the air, I'm sure we would have seen one. This, of course, was a North American, as opposed to a European beaver. To tell the truth, there is very little difference between them apart from size, the American, as you would expect, being slightly bigger than its European counterpart.

As we approached the lower Tazemna Lake, we saw a magnificent bald eagle, America's national bird, perched regally on the top of one of the tallest pines. It was an adult bird, with its white head and tail, and black body, and it dwarfed the magpie that was bold (or foolish) enough to mob it.

As if the rafting wasn't enough exercise for one day, in the evening, Ceri and I walked the few miles to Tanalian Falls in the shadow of Tanalian Mountain. The falls proved to be very picturesque but nothing could compensate for the four pints of blood we lost to the dreaded mosquitoes. I made a mental note not to venture out in the evening again.

August 14th To continue the outdoor theme, we spent the day fishing on some of the tributary rivers pouring into Lake Clark. To my amazement, the whole family enjoyed the experience as we sped along the open water on an aluminium boat, stopping occasionally to fish or sunbathe.

The first port of call was the mouth of the Tanalian river where we were put to shame by Jeff, one of our guides. We had been fishing for over an hour to no avail when Jeff caught two beautiful grayling with just two casts. Mind you, he had used a bait that mimicked a salmon egg drifting down river while the rest of us used spinners that mimicked small fish. Whatever the reason for Jeff's success, we moved on to a shallow part of the lake where Ceri, her father and Dewi managed to catch sizeable pike. There are some monsters in the lake but the biggest of those we caught was probably around seven pounds in weight.

Pike are the great white sharks of lakes and ponds. They have hundreds of sharp teeth in a huge, gaping mouth and they will devour virtually anything from small fish to frogs, ducklings, small mammals and even sizeable ducks on occasion. They are also superbly well-camouflaged and they have an incredible turn of speed that they use when ambushing prey. Every fish we caught was put back and I'm ashamed to say that I didn't catch a single one. It must have been the bait I was given . . .

August 15th Our last full day in Port Alsworth and it was spent flying around the lakes and mountains in search of mammals and birds we hadn't previously seen. We landed on a small lake where Glen had previously watched bald eagles and ospreys fishing and, sure enough, as we ate our packed lunch, two ospreys circled overhead. This panicked a group of several hundred ducks that retreated into the thick vegetation along the water's edge but the ospreys had eyes only for the fish.

After two aborted attempts, one of the ospreys finally managed to plunge into the water to catch a sizeable pike but as it gained height, it was mobbed by the second bird. It released the fish and turned its attention to the second osprey but the interference proved too much for both birds because they then drifted slowly westwards, presumably to fish separately at different lakes. It's strange to think that in Scotland, and now in Wales, we make a huge fuss about a bird of prey that has such a widespread distribution from Australia to Canada. There again, when you've only got one pair, I suppose all the attention is justified.

Hundreds of American robins were flocking together in the spruce woodlands in order to migrate south but the trumpeter and tundra swans still had youngsters in tow and it will be more than a month before they think about migrating to warmer climes. We searched in vain for moose but despite flying over thousands of acres of suitable marshy habitat, we didn't see any.

On the return journey to Port Alsworth, we flew around the peak of Tanalian Mountain where we saw over a dozen dall sheep. These are truly wild sheep, much prized by hunters, that feed only on the highest and most inaccessible ledges. Up here above the treeline, we also saw several black bears, some with cubs, feeding on the glut of berries. Although it was only mid-August, the leaves on some of the higher birch trees were already turning brown. Winter comes early in Alaska.

August 18th Two days ago, with heavy hearts, we packed our bags to leave wonderful Port Alsworth with its memorable scenery, fantastic wildlife and welcoming people, so that we could return to Anchorage

LAKE CLARK

and then move on to New York. As we walked around the edge of Lake Clark for one last time, a pair of ravens circled overhead and a Pacific loon, better known to us as a great northern diver, paddled effortlessly through the misty waters. It had been a magical few days in one of the world's last true wild areas.

Manhattan was different. It had its usual gathering of sickly pigeons as well as starlings and house sparrows, both introduced by the early European settlers. Some of the bigger parks also had substantial populations of grey squirrels, this time a native species, but the highlight for me was seeing a bright orange monarch butterfly flying through Times Square. These amazing insects migrate south from the United States to spend the winter months in one small valley in Mexico where hundreds of millions gather together, so seeing one in the middle of a large city probably wasn't too unusual.

For me, the few days spent in New York were very unpleasant because of the noise and the millions of people. I was amazed by the number of obese Americans, but as no one appears to walk anywhere and everyone eats huge meals, I can't say I was very surprised. It's a shame more of them don't walk around some of their beautiful parks to enjoy the wildlife and the cleaner air.

August 22nd We finally arrived home on my birthday and driving through Wales reminded me of just how beautiful this country is. There is nothing like a few weeks in a foreign country to remind us of that fact.

On the way home, I saw that very little had changed in my absence although all the roadside hogweed had gone to seed and even the ragwort and rosebay willowherb were well past their best. Bramble flowers had given way to dark, ripe blackberries so I'll have to gather some when I get home and ask my mum to bake a tart. Her blackberry and apple tarts are just about the best in the world.

At home, I walked the dogs around the fields at the back of the house where I was surprised to find a newly-fledged group of young sparrowhawks in a nearby woodland. I had walked along the edge of the wood several times in the spring but I had never seen one of these elusive raptors. Now, with the young begging for food, they were very obvious, if a little late in fledging. With the abundance of small woodland birds, they should do well.

August 23rd My wife and I celebrated our eighth wedding anniversary with a lie-in until 10 o'clock and then, as it was my first full day back in Wales, it was time to take the dogs for a proper walk. We went along the river Severn east of Newtown to revisit some regular haunts, including a long, narrow field that's lightly grazed by horses.

The alder and sycamores along the banks of the river echoed to the sounds of alarm-calling long-tailed tits and nuthatches despite the fact that the dogs and I posed no threat whatsoever, whilst a lone great spotted woodpecker flicked bark from a rotting ash in search of invertebrate prey. This species has had an excellent year and I have seen breeding pairs in all kinds of habitats throughout Wales, particularly along the edges of conifer plantations.

It will be difficult to go back to work after Alaska but at least I have one more day of rest.

August 25th I left home early this morning to film around Blaenau Ffestiniog in north-west Wales, a town that has a reputation of being a wet, miserable and grey location. It is, in fact, a great place for wildlife with its slate quarries full of choughs and rare ferns and the moorlands that support breeding hen harriers, merlin and grouse. We actually filmed along a gorge called Ceunant Cynfal that has a series of tumbling waterfalls, some ancient oaks and incredible scenery. The cascading

CHOUGH (photo: Steve Phillipps)

water means that there is plenty of humidity in the air throughout the year to support the healthy populations of ferns and mosses that cover the rocks and tree trunks like Axminster carpets. I'm sure any botanist worth his salt would have a field day here!

August 26th Another day near Blaenau Ffestiniog, but this time we were filming on the edge of the Migneint moor. Whilst August is not the best time to see birds on the moor, on the rocky outcrops, the bright yellow gorse flowers looked stunning against the purple heather and in one very wet area, I managed to find a single bog asphodel still in flower, about a month later than its neighbours which were all in seed.

Sundew and butterwort, two plants that have adapted to the nutrient-poor environment by becoming carnivorous, were abundant, and as we walked through the wetter areas, we disturbed several frogs. Golden-ringed dragonflies patrolled the upper reaches of the Cynfal river in search of insect prey and both buzzards and kestrels hovered overhead in search of small mammals. Did I just say that the moors were fairly quiet in August? I was wrong.

August 27th I had a brilliant day today, flying like a bird off a hill in the middle of Radnorshire! I had never been paragliding before and therefore I had to go in tandem with Tim, an expert who holds the world record for travelling over 400 miles in one jump. I was perfectly happy to travel 400 kilometres from the top of the hill down to the bottom, narrowly missing some gorse bushes as we landed.

A good paraglider has to be an excellent naturalist because it is only by watching the movement of birds that one finds out what the wind is doing. At first, we saw very few birds in the air but gradually, as the wind lifted, swallows and house martins began to work their way up to the hilltop in search of insects. Soon, buzzards and ravens could be seen wheeling overhead and we knew it was time for that one huge leap. Pumping my legs as fast as I could, within seconds, we were airborne. What a feeling! We'd gone from a few seconds of adrenaline-charged activity to perfect peace. It was like sitting in a comfortable armchair with buzzards and ravens as companions.

The flight may only have lasted about five minutes but it was a glorious experience for me to get as close as a human being can get to flying like a bird. I felt every ounce of air pressure and turbulence, every sudden shift in wind direction and it's only now that I truly understand why soaring birds occasionally flick their tails or subtly angle their wings as they glide along a hillside. I'll have to try it again – soon!

August 29th This morning, I walked around the village with the boys and the dogs and counted the numbers of house martin nests that had been used this year. Last year, 12 nests had been occupied and a lad who has lived in the village all his life says that he had counted at least 26 pairs in the hot summer of 1976. This year has been quite a poor one for this species and this was reflected in the fact that I could find only four nests. I had counted the nests in late June also and come up with the same number but I was hoping that one or two late pairs would have attempted to breed this year. Some nests are undoubtedly knocked down illegally by people who don't want to have to clean up after the birds but most people I spoke to welcome the birds and are sad to see them disappear.

In the afternoon, I visited a good friend who was visiting his childhood home, a farm on the outskirts of Llanfyllin. I used to cycle over from Llanwddyn to visit Hugh Gately and his family and even now, 30 years later, I always make an effort to visit him when he returns to the area. The farm, Glyn Engyll, is completely organic and they cut late hay rather than silage. The fields, even this late in the year, are full of flowers such as small scabious and eyebright and it's the only site in Montgomeryshire that still has glow-worms. Their outbuildings are full of swallows and at least seven pairs of house martins nest under their eaves. I just wish there were more farms like this around the countryside because the farmer, the family, the livestock and the wildlife reap the benefits.

In the early evening, I walked along the Montgomeryshire Canal as far as Pwll Penarth, a nature reserve on the outskirts of Newtown. The guelder-rose, elders and brambles were heavy with berries and all the badger latrines were full of purple droppings because the animals had been gorging on the abundant blackberries. It's not such a good year for conkers or nuts, however, although there are still plenty of grey squirrels around.

On the canal, I met up with Hissing Sid, his mate and five youngsters and I bumped into a local lady who told me that only last week, Sid had chased off a group of five heavily-built ramblers. Sid is actually a pussycat at heart but you really do not want to meet him on one of his off days.

August 30th There's nothing quite like filming in glorious sunshine amongst the mountains of Snowdonia. Today, the crew and I walked from Capel Curig, through the blooming gorse and heather, through Cwm Crafnant, and down towards the village of Trefriw. It's a wonderful mosaic of open moorland, deciduous and coniferous woodland, rocky outcrops and bogs, and because of this variety of habitats, it's a great place for wildlife.

Ravens were constant companions, as were sheep and ramblers, but the former were far more entertaining with their acrobatics and deep kronking calls. Buzzards, too, were taking advantage of the thermals rising off the exposed rock surfaces and the begging calls of youngsters echoed through the surrounding oak woods. Flocks of redpoll and siskin were flitting from tree to tree in search of seeds amongst the birch woodlands, a sure sign that autumn is knocking on our door. Goldcrests, winter visitors from the far north, were also busily searching for insects amongst the bark and ivy-clad branches of the oaks

The highlight of the day was watching golden-ringed dragonflies chasing each other along a mountain stream, each one defending its own territory and hunting for insects along the banks. While we watched, one of the females began to lay eggs by hovering and flicking her tail into the water, laying one egg each time. She then moved on to the next section of open water before repeating the process.
Underneath a flat rock on the riverbed, I found a dragonfly nymph, a beast of a creature about three centimetres in length, that hunts other invertebrates along the stream bed. Eventually, it will climb out of the water, anchor itself on a plant stem and split along its back to allow an adult dragonfly to emerge. Even up in the tiniest of streams in the high ground of Snowdonia, miracles abound.

August 31st The swallows were gathering along telegraph wires and tree branches as I drove down to south Wales this morning and clouds of both swallows and house martins were frantically hoovering up insects from the moor above Fochriw in preparation for their return journey to Africa. Another glorious summer is drawing to a close and winter already has one foot in the door.

Today was another tandem paragliding day with Tim, my experienced pilot. This time, however, I was in for some serious paragliding as we were hoping to fly with three captive-bred red kites and getting it right for the camera crew could take some time. We gauged the strength and direction of the wind and the presence or absence of thermals largely from the buzzards and ravens that kept us company throughout the day. A family of kestrels hunted continuously along the ridge, diving occasionally on a beetle or a vole that would provide a tasty mouthful.

I tried to tempt the kites to fly alongside by waving some bait in my hands. The young kites, however, were suspicious of the paraglider, hanging like some enormous phantom overhead, and it quickly became apparent that it would be some time yet before they became accustomed to this new creature. Never mind, at least it gives me one more opportunity to enjoy paragliding.

It's difficult to believe that a whole year has passed since I first put finger to keyboard to record a year of wildlife in Wales and throughout the world. The year has seen me travel to all four corners of the Earth to see some of nature's many miracles, but it has also been another year full of reminders that Wales is truly a remarkable country. It is compact but full to the brim with a myriad of habitats supporting an incredible variety of wildlife. Those of us who live here are blessed and those who visit, however briefly, are privileged. It is a living countryside that is engrained in our history and in our souls and it is what makes us what we are. Let's ensure that it's there for future generations to enjoy.

YOUNG GREAT SPOTTED WOODPECKER (photo: Steve Phillipps)